DISC VER DELHI

THE CITY'S HISTORY & CULTURE REDEFINED

Anjana Motihar Chandra

Marshall Cavendish
Editions

Series Editor: Melvin Neo
Designer: Benson Tan
Picture Research: Thomas Khoo

All photos by Pietro Scozzari except pages 17, 160 (Government of India Tourist Office);
page 59 (Bes Stock); pages 115, 131 (AFP); page 157 (Lonely Planet Images)

This publication represents the opinions and views of the author based on her personal
experience, knowledge and research. The information in this book serves as a general
guide only. The reader is advised to consult a medical doctor, clinical nutritionist or
professional trainer before starting any form of treatment or exercise. The author and
publisher have used their best efforts in preparing this book and disclaim liability rising
directly and indirectly from the use and application of this book.

Other Marshall Cavendish Offices:
Marshall Cavendish Ltd. 5th Floor, 32-38 Saffron Hill, London EC1N 8 FH, UK •
Marshall Cavendish Corporation. 99 White Plains Road, Tarrytown NY 10591-9001,
USA • Marshall Cavendish International (Thailand) Co Ltd. 253 Asoke, 12th Flr,
Sukhumvit 21 Road, Klongtoey Nua, Wattana, Bangkok 10110, Thailand • Marshall
Cavendish (Malaysia) Sdn Bhd, Times Subang, Lot 46, Subang Hi-Tech Industrial
Park, Batu Tiga, 40000 Shah Alam, Selangor Darul Ehsan, Malaysia

Marshall Cavendish is a trademark of Times Publishing Limited

National Library Board Singapore Cataloguing in Publication Data

Chandra, Anjana Motihar, 1959-
Discover Delhi : the city's history & culture redefined / Anjana Motihar Chandra. –
Singapore : Marshall Cavendish Editions, c2008.
p. cm.
Includes index.
ISBN-13 : 978-981-261-518-3 (pbk.)
ISBN-10 : 981-261-518-0 (pbk.)

1. Historic buildings – India – Delhi. 2. Delhi (India) – Social life and customs.
3. Delhi (India) – History. 4. Delhi (India) – Miscellanea. I. Title.

DS486.D3
954.56 — dc22   OCN191921727

Printed in Singapore by Times Graphics Pte Ltd

CONTENTS

SUBJECT INDEX

🌸 Cultural Interest

❤️ Lifestyle

PREFACE

Delhi is a unique city of contrasts, where the ancient and modern, wealth and poverty, gardens and congested markets, bureaucracy and industry stand harmoniously side by side within its vast 1,483 sq km geographic area. With its remarkable treasure trove of about 1,200 historic monuments, two of them World Heritage sites, and the melange of cultures and communities among its almost 14 million people, Delhi presents an ideal starting point for a journey into India and its fascinating past.

Delhi's strategic location on the trade route with central Asia in medieval times made it an ideal choice as the seat of power for the diverse dynasties that ruled India centuries ago. However, while Delhi's history dates back to 1,000 BC, it was only in the 11th century AD that it came into prominence with Lal Kot, the first of its seven cities, established by the Tomar clan of the Rajput warrior community. The wealth and opulence of the region attracted Muslim invaders who by 1206 had founded the all-powerful Delhi Sultanate which ruled the vast Indian subcontinent until the Mughals took control in 1526. Under Mughal emperor Shah Jahan in the 17th century, Delhi was at the pinnacle of its architectural splendour, epitomised by Shah Jahan's magnificent Lal Qila (Red Fort) and Jama Masjid, and his capital city Shahjahanabad, now old Delhi. Sovereignty returned to Delhi when the British created New Delhi, the imperial capital of their 'Jewel of the British Crown', with broad tree-lined avenues and open spaces, a foil to the narrow, congested streets of adjacent old Delhi.

In 1947, Delhi became the capital of a free India and has since retained its pre-eminent position in the Indian union. In the ensuing years, the city has grown to become the National Capital Region with satellite towns such as Noida and Gurgaon under its purview. Where once the city primarily encompassed bustling old Delhi and British New Delhi, today, it stretches far and wide from north to south, east to west, a conglomerate of teeming colonies with the Yamuna River snaking through its centre. In the 21st century, Delhi, the third largest city in India, is brimming over with people, swank new residential and commercial buildings, markets and malls, juxtaposed with shanty towns and streets choking with the fumes of expensive foreign cars.

But even as the city grows in size, population and affluence, it remains rooted to its rich heritage, vestiges of which are visible in its enduring medieval monuments and imposing colonial buildings, and its lush green *char bagh* gardens harking back to the Mughal days. Delhi's museums also tell a spellbinding tale, beginning with the ancient Indus Valley Civilisation and culminating in the 20th century nationalist movement of Mahatma Gandhi and Jawaharlal Nehru, which was a precursor to India's independence.

This book attempts to unravel the old and new face of Delhi, delving into its unique antecedents while chronicling the modern-day lifestyle of its people. Tombs, palaces, forts, gardens, films, fashion, culture, cuisines, cricket, crafts and books are all discussed in this exhaustive study of India's singular capital city.

Anjana Motihar Chandra
Spring 2008

ART GALLERIES

Art has become big business in India as more and more affluent Indians invest hundreds and thousands of rupees on works by contemporary masters with the promise of profitable returns. Buyer interest has shifted from miniature paintings, sculptures and traditional folk and tribal creations to modern art, causing a mushrooming of galleries in all major Indian cities to cater to the demand. Delhi, a leader in the business, has over 70 galleries including a number of pre-eminent national-level art establishments. Besides, many distinguished artists such as Anjolie Ela Menon, Satish Gujral and Jatin Das reside and work in the city, which is especially abuzz with activity in the winter months, the period from October to March that is its primary art and cultural season.

A young sculptor giving vent to his creative instincts at the Garhi Studio.

Standing tall among the plethora of art establishments in Delhi is the National Gallery of Modern Art (NGMA), a premier institution which has an outstanding collection of 15,000 paintings, graphics and sculptures dating from the 1850s to present day. The gallery showcases the development of international and national art through the ages and regularly holds retrospective shows of foreign and Indian artists. Among its notable Indian works are the towering Triumph of Labour sculpture by Devi Prasad Roy Choudhary, the painting Lady in Moonlight by Raja Ravi Verma and Flowerface by Abanidranath Tagore. Other eminent artists from India whose works are on display here are Rabindranath Tagore, Nandalal Bose, Jamini Roy and Amrita Sher-Gil, and from the United Kingdom, Henry Moore and Jacob Epstein.

The Lalit Kala Akademi is a state-owned gallery that aims to promote visual arts in the country. Since its first national exhibition in 1958, it has gone on to hold countless showings of upcoming Indian artists, sometimes holding several simultaneously. It also conducts the annual National Exhibition of Contemporary Art and the esteemed Triennale India, a showing of international art, on its premises at Rabindra Bhawan in central Delhi. The Lalit Kala Akademi is headquartered in Delhi and has five regional centres, including the Garhi Studio in south Delhi where promising artists are provided complete studio facilities so they can give full rein to their creative instincts.

LOCATION:
All over Delhi, notably the central and south zones.

Workshops and lectures are regularly held here, and visitors may be able to pick up a freshly painted canvas at a bargain price.

Triveni Kala Sangam, known simply as Triveni, is a quaint cultural complex with four galleries, a sculpture court, an open-air auditorium, bookshop and cafeteria. The largest gallery in this complex, popular with the arty set, intellectuals and students, is Shridharani Gallery which showcases established as well as upcoming artists. Art Heritage in the basement, founded by costume designer and author Roshen Alkazi, exhibits eminent artists and organises interactive workshops.

Other active galleries in Delhi include the Dhoomimal Art Gallery, one of the oldest in the city which also has a branch called the Dhoomimal Art Centre; Gallerie Ganesha, known for encouraging young talent; Gallery Espace; Visual Arts Gallery at the India Habitat Centre, which presents an eclectic mix of art works; the Vadehra Art Gallery, known for its permanent collections of eminent artists such as Maqbool Fida Husain and Ram Kumar; the Village Gallery and Delhi Art Gallery, both in Hauz Khas Village; India International Centre (IIC), a leading cultural and conference centre where exhibitions are held periodically (see Lodhi Garden, page 86); and the All India Fine Arts and Crafts Society (AIFACS), a cultural centre which also organises exhibitions.

Delhi's umpteen galleries offer an eclectic mix of modern and traditional art.

AUTORICKSHAWS

Autorickshaws, a type of taxi, are a cheap way to travel around Delhi, although the ride can get bumpy because of the lightweight design of this three-wheeled vehicle. The autorickshaw is a motorised version of the traditional cycle rickshaw, a bicycle- or tricycle-driven buggy that can seat two people. In the case of the autorickshaw, a scooter with a two-stroke engine and handlebars drives the vehicle.

While the cycle rickshaw is usually found in old Delhi, being banned from Connaught Place and other central Delhi areas, the autorickshaw is available throughout the city and can be flagged down on the road. Autorickshaws can be found in most Indian towns and cities as well as neighbouring nations such as Nepal, Pakistan and Bangladesh. Vehicles of a similar type, called *tuk tuk*, are found in Thailand, Laos and Cambodia.

The autorickshaw or 'auto' as it is popularly referred to in Delhi, is black and yellow or black and green in colour with a covered top and back, and open sides with a canvas flap. There is a single passenger seat inside which can accommodate two to three people, and the driver sits in a single seat in front. The vehicle is powered by either petrol or compressed natural gas (CNG). It was in July 1998 that the Supreme Court of India ordered the Delhi government to convert all public transport vehicles to CNG to reduce the dangerous levels of pollution, a move that has improved the quality of Delhi air. The maximum speed of the autorickshaw is about 50 km per hour, though most travel at about 35 km per hour.

The vehicle is fitted with a meter which records the distance travelled according to the prevailing rate per kilometre. However, autorickshaw drivers are notorious for fleecing passengers by claiming their meters don't work. In many cases, the driver may simply prefer not to put the meter on, which allows him to charge at will. In such a situation, visitors to Delhi need to ask for the tariff chart, mandatory for all drivers to carry, which clearly spells out the fare according to the distance travelled. If this is not available, a rate suitable to both parties can be negotiated at the outset.

AYURVEDA AND YOGA

Nature cures and herbal remedies have existed in India since the ancient Vedic civilisation. Among the most popular of these systems is Ayurveda, known for its holistic outlook and natural healing, and yoga for its health enhancng properties. The two have come together in wellness centres throughout the country which offer them as a cure-all for an entire spectrum of ailments.

Ayurveda

Ayurveda, which is the Sanskrit for 'meaning or knowledge of life', is said to have divine origins, having been delivered to humanity by the Hindu God Brahma, the supreme creator. In the Ayurveda system of medicine, human beings, and all objects in the Universe, consist of five elements—space, air, fire, water and earth—with two or more of these combining to produce specific reactions. For instance, space and air combine to form *vata dosha* which directs nerve impulses, circulation, respiration and elimination in the human body, while water and earth combine to form *kapha dosha* which controls growth.

Each individual is made up of unique proportions of *vata*, *pitta* and *kapha* and their imbalance can cause illness. Ayurvedic treatments, which depend heavily on oil massage and use ingredients such as turmeric, sulphur, iron, powdered dried fruit and tree root as medication, help to restore the balance. An Ayurvedic treatment could include pouring a continuous stream of medicinal oil on the head and body during an hour-long vigorous massage, rubbing oil on the body with a cotton cloth or instilling medicated oil into the nostrils. These are designed to improve blood circulation and enhance the function of vital organs.

Yoga

Yoga, which aims to achieve a perfect balance between the body and mind through a combination of bodily postures, breathing exercises and meditation, originated in the ancient Vedic period, but was given a formal structure by the sage Patanjali, called the Father of Yoga, in circa 200 BC. At the heart of Patanjali's philosophy was the eightfold yogic path, or ashtanga yoga, for all-round development leading to the ultimate goal of the union of the individual soul with the Universal Spirit.

Pouring medicinal oil on the head in a continuous stream is one of myriad Ayurvedic treatments.

The eight, known as the eight limbs of Patanjali are: Yama (abstentions) with the five yamas being non-violence, truth, abstention from theft, continence, abstention from possessions; Niyama (observances) which are purity, contentment, austerity, self-study and living with an awareness of the divine; Asana (postures); Pranayama (breath control); Pratyahara (sense control); Dharana (concentration); Dhyana (meditation); and Samadhi (absolute bliss). Yoga does not use any drugs but through its practices helps develop full efficiency of the various organs of the body, particularly the excretory and urinary systems through which all the harmful toxins are eliminated.

Yoga maintains a perfect balance between the body and mind through a combination of breathing exercises and meditation.

BAHA'I **HOUSE** OF **WORSHIP**

An exotic half open lotus flower created in concrete and marble is the symbol of the resplendent Baha'i House of Worship, popularly known as the Lotus Temple, in Delhi. This temple dedicated to the Baha'i faith can be found at the extreme southern end of the city, in a lavish setting of water pools and gardens in which the lotus appears to be floating.

The Lotus Temple, a mammoth international project, took almost seven years to construct. It was opened on 24 December 1986 and since then has been attracting millions of visitors every year, with devotees from all religions free to pray or meditate here according to their particular faiths. There are no idols in this house of worship, nor are any rituals conducted here. A 15-minute prayer service is held four times a day during which selections from different holy books are read out. Audiovisual

LOCATION:
Bahapur Kalkaji, south Delhi. Website: http://www. bahaindia.org/ temple
Closed on Monday.

presentations about the Baha'i faith are also held at regular intervals during the day.

The building of the Baha'i Temple in Delhi had an international essence with creative talent as well as raw materials sourced from all over the world. For instance, the marble used to cover the petals was quarried from the Mount Pentitikon mines in Greece and cut in Italy, and the concrete came from Korea. The building's architect Fariborz Sahba, a Canadian citizen and a Baha'i of Iranian descent also epitomises this global spirit.

In the magnificent Lotus Temple, nine-sided like other Baha'i houses of worship to symbolise the diversity and unity of the human race, the 27 marble-clad petals are arranged in layers with the exterior tier of petals, nine in all, opening outwards to form the different entrances to the outer hall. The next set of nine petals, which appear partly closed, rise above to form the main structure which holds the central hall. Nine doors open into this central prayer hall which has a capacity to hold 2,500 people. Adding to the ethereal façade of the blooming petals are the surrounding pools of water, nine in all. The number nine has special significance in the Baha'i faith, being the highest single-digit number symbolising completeness.

The lotus flower was chosen for the Baha'i House of Worship because of the special place it holds in different religions, including Hinduism where the creator Brahma is said to have sprung from the lotus flower. The lotus is also the national flower of India. Mr Sahba travelled across India to carry out research for the temple design and finally settled on the lotus as representing the unity of all religions. This maxim is at the foundation of the Baha'i religion which also advocates oneness of God, oneness of mankind and worship over rituals. The religion was founded in Iran in the 19th century by Persian nobleman Bahá'u'lláh.

The Delhi Lotus Temple is the seventh of the major Baha'i houses of worship built around the world, and has won several prestigious engineering and design awards from such notable groups as the American Institute of Architects and the Institution of Structural Engineers of the UK. The other six Baha'i temples are: Wilmette, Illinois in the United States; Kampala, Uganda; Sydney (Ingleside), Australia; Frankfurt (Langenhain-Hofheim), Germany; Panama City, Panama; and Tiapapata, Samoa.

BANGLA SAHIB **GURDWARA**

The Bangla Sahib Gurdwara is a striking 18th century Sikh shrine in central Delhi that draws devotees all year round.

With its prominent golden dome and marble edifice, Bangla Sahib is easily recognisable as Delhi's most important *gurdwara* or Sikh house of worship. Located in central Delhi near Gole Dak Khana, Bangla Sahib Gurdwara stands on the site of a bungalow where Guru Har Krishan, the eighth Sikh guru, resided during a visit to Delhi in 1664.

The bungalow belonged to Indian leader Raja Jai Singh Amber, and Guru Har Krishan was his guest at a time when a Sikh succession struggle was underway. During his stay in Delhi, a smallpox and cholera epidemic broke out in the city and Guru Har Krishan helped heal ill and suffering residents by giving them fresh water from a well, said to have been blessed by him, located in the bungalow grounds. The water from the well is considered sacred even today and is distributed to devotees as holy water.

The Bangla Sahib Gurdwara was built at the site by a Sikh devotee, Sardar Baghel Singh, in 1783. In the 20th century, Baba Harbans Singh made extensive additions to the building. Besides the well, the *gurdwara* complex has a school, an art gallery, a bathing pond or *sarovar*, and a large kitchen where the traditonal *langar* or free vegetarian meal for devotees visiting the temple is prepared. The Delhi Sikh Gurdwara Management Committee also runs a small charitable hospital in the basement of the Bangla Sahib Gurdwara building.

As in all Sikh and Hindu temples, visitors are required to remove their shoes at the entrance and enter the holy premises barefoot. At Bangla Sahib and other Sikh temples, visitors are also required to cover their heads with a scarf or piece of cloth as a mark of respect to the holy Sikh book, the *Guru Granth Sahib*, which occupies a small pavilion at the centre of the inner chamber. Scarfs are available at the entrance for visitors who don't have a head covering.

Hymns from the *Granth Sahib* are sung throughout the day, beginning before sunrise and ending at 9pm when the holy book is put away for the night after an elaborate ritual.

LOCATION:
Off Ashoka Road, near Gol Dak Khana. One kilometre from Connaught Place. Nearest Metro Station: Patel Chowk

BOOK**SHOPS**

Indians love to read, whether it is magazines, newspapers or books. In fact, according to the NOP World Culture Score Index (2005), Indians are the world's most voracious readers, reading an average 10.9 hours a week, twice as much as Americans. Interestingly, India, which publishes books in 24 languages, is the third largest publisher of English books in the world after the United States and the United Kingdom. As many as 70,000 new titles are published in the country every year of which 20,000 are in English.

For their daily book reading fix, Delhi residents visit libraries, bookshops, pavement stalls and second-hand booksellers. Most of the latest international bestsellers are available in the city shortly after their launch overseas. Since these books are usually reprints by Indian publishers, their prices tend to be much lower than international editions, which make them especially attractive for foreign tourists looking for a good bargain.

There are a number of bookshops scattered throughout Delhi, but the best ones are found in central and south Delhi. Among the more popular stores in the Connaught Place area are The Bookworm, E.D Galgotia & Sons and the English Book Store, while there is Bahri Sons and the Times Book Gallery in Khan Market, a few kilometres away. Bahri Sons, which opened its doors in 1950, a few years after the partition of the Indian subcontinent, prides itself on its large collection of fiction and non-fiction books, and for being able to acquire "any title published anywhere in India" for its customers.

In the southern part of the city, there is Teksons, Midlands, and Om Book Shop, some with multiple branches. There are also specialist stores like Fact and Fiction in Vasant Vihar which has a wide collection of books on international affairs and languages, and Full Circle in Khan Market, which specialises in books on spirituality and self-help.

Shopping malls in the outskirts of Delhi, in Noida and Gurgaon, also have noteworthy bookshops such as Crossword, one of a chain of over 40 throughout the country. Crossword claims to be a lifestyle bookstore offering reading corners and cafes in its large premises, unlike the others which are largely traditional shops, providing books and stationery in a compact

LOCATION:
All over Delhi, notably Connaught Place and Khan Market

space. However, many of these traditional bookshops have gone online in the Internet-driven 21st century, and are supplying books based on orders made on their websites. Some are even offering to deliver in other countries.

Offering hefty discounts and even second-hand books at throwaway prices are pavement stalls in the inner circle of Connaught Place, and in some of the other markets in central and south Delhi. These stalls also sell old and new magazines. For books that are out of print, there is Nai Sarak in Chandni Chowk, old Delhi, one of the largest markets of its kind in the city. Another good place to buy books is a fair, with the annual Delhi Book Fair and the New Delhi World Book Fair, a mega international event organised biennially by the National Book Trust usually in the month of February, being huge draws.

BUDDHA JAYANTI PARK
AND THE RIDGE

A sculpture of the Buddha looks benignly over Buddha Jayanti Park, an expansive park near the diplomatic enclave Chanakyapuri in the middle of Delhi's green belt, called the Ridge. The Ridge is undulating terrain covered by dense scrub forest, referred to as the 'lungs of the city' since it is the only open area in Delhi's overpopulated concrete jungle.

The Ridge was barren rocky land, dotted with thorny scrub until Delhi Emperor Firoz Shah Tughlaq (r.1351-1388) transformed a section of it into a hunting arena. He erected an enclosure for game and built the Kushak Jahan Numa hunting lodge, later called Pir Ghaib after a mystic who disappeared while meditating there. The ruins of Pir Ghaib and a step well are located near present-day Hindu Rao Hospital in north Delhi. Firoz Shah also erected a 3rd century BC Ashoka Pillar, one of two he had transported to Delhi, at the lodge.

The Ridge is also associated with the Sepoy Mutiny of 1857. British forces, camped at its northern end during the uprising, attacked from there the mutineers hiding in the city. Flagstaff Tower, strategically located on the Ridge, was the spot where British women and children waited for help before fleeing the city. The British declared the Ridge a Reserved Forest in 1878 and planted a profusion of indigenous trees there. Neem, which provides dense cover and is acclaimed for its medicinal properties, was planted extensively, as was Kikar or Babul.

Pipal or Bodhi trees can be found in abundance at Buddha Jayanti Park as it was under the Bodhi tree that Siddhartha Gautama, the founder of Buddhism, attained enlightenment. The statue of Buddha was installed on a sandstone pavilion in the park in 1993 by the 14th Dalai Lama Tenzin Gyatso, the spiritual leader of the Tibetan people. Every year, Buddhist devotees celebrate Vesak, known as Buddha Poornima or Buddha Jayanti in India, at Buddha Jayanti Park. This day, falling in April or May, is most auspicious for Buddhists because it commemorates the birth, enlightenment and death of the Buddha.

A note of caution for visitors: Buddha Jayanti Park does not have a good safety record, being located in a secluded area, so visitors are advised to be careful while they are there.

LOCATION:
Ridge Road, near Dhaula Kuan and Rajinder Nagar.

BUKHARA **RESTAURANT**

When it comes to *tandoori* chicken, *naan* and other Mughlai delicacies, few restaurants can compare with Bukhara, in Maurya Sheraton Hotel. This highly sought-after restaurant in one of Delhi's leading five-star hotels lays claim to having the best Mughlai and Frontier food (see Mughlai Cuisine, page 104) in the city. But Bukhara's reputation seems to have traversed far beyond the narrow city limits of the Indian capital. According to the prestigious *Restaurant* magazine based in the United Kingdom, Bukhara is the best restaurant in India, as well as in Asia.

The magazine's S.Pellegrino World's 50 Best Restaurants ranking, compiled by the Nespresso World's 50 Best Academy, a group of eminent culinary experts and critics, selected Bukhara as the best restaurant in Asia in 2007, and 37th worldwide. It is the only restaurant from India to feature in this prestigious list, and has done so thrice since 2004.

So what makes Bukhara so special? It has a rugged ambience to recreate the environment of the North West Frontier Province of Pakistan, from where it draws its inspiration. Greeting guests to the Bukhara are walls made of hard rock, wooden columns and a wooden ceiling, copper pans for decoration, low tables with stools and an open-display kitchen with *tandoor* clay ovens, where the chefs work hard preparing dinner.

The cuisine, prepared by top chefs, is singular in taste and quality and presented on a novel wooden menu. The range of *tandoori* items, that has not changed since the restaurant was opened almost 30 years ago, includes succulent kebabs, mutton chops, *tikkas*, *tandoori* fish, chicken and prawn, as well as its pièce de résistance, the *sikankari raan*, which is the whole leg of a spring lamb marinated in a variety of spices and cooked in the *tandoor*. There are also plenty of vegetarian *tandoori* dishes and a variety of *naans* and breads on offer.

Bukhara's management reveals proudly that world leaders and dignitaries have dined at the restaurant. They include Bill Clinton and his daughter Chelsea, Tony Blair, Microsoft Chairman Bill Gates and rock legend Mick Jagger. In memory of the Clintons, Bukhara has named one of its non-vegetarian dishes the President's Platter and a vegetarian dish, Chelsea's Platter.

CENTRAL COTTAGE INDUSTRIES EMPORIUM AND STATE EMPORIUMS

India has a rich tradition of handicrafts and handlooms and there is no better place to experience these exquisite products made by skilled artisans than at the government-run emporiums in Connaught Place, central Delhi.

Taking centrestage is the Central Cottage Industries Emporium, or the Cottage as it is popularly known, the government's flagship store. It sells crafts from across the country under one roof. Representing the different states in the Indian union are the smaller state emporiums which offer handcrafted items that are distinctive of their respective regions. While the Cottage is located in Jawapar Vyapar Bhawan on Janpath, the state emporiums are about a kilometre away on Baba Kharak Singh Marg.

The Cottage, established in 1948, is a popular one-stop shop for tourists looking for gifts or souvenirs of their holiday in India. It has a remarkable range of furniture, carpets, paintings, pottery, glassware, brass, wood, silver objects and jewellery, textiles and much more within its massive 3,345 sq m showroom spread over

LOCATION:

Cottage: Jawahar Vyapar Bhawan, Janpath
Tel: 23326790/ 23320439
Website: http://www.cottage emporiumindia.com/home.asp
Open daily.
Nearest Metro Station: Patel Chowk

State Emporiums: Baba Kharak Singh Marg. Closed on Sunday.
Nearest Metro Station: Rajiv Chowk.

The Cottage and State Emporiums have an exhaustive collection of high quality handcrafted items at fixed prices.

eight floors. All the items are created by skilled artisans trained in the traditional arts, so both quality and workmanship are assured. Prices are fixed and there is no haggling here.

Prices are fixed at the 18 state emporiums on Baba Kharak Singh Marg too. These emporiums offer a unique opportunity to explore the fascinating craft traditions of Indian states without having to travel. Each region is distinguished by its own unique designs and craftsmanship even though the raw material may be similar. The Kashmir emporium boasts of the carpets and shawls the state is famous for as well as its colourful lacquerwork; the southern states of Tamil Nadu and Kerala showcase brass lamps and wooden statues; while Rajasthan and Gujarat entice visitors with embroidered ethnic attire, cushion covers and quilts. Rajasthan is also acclaimed for its leather, colourful wooden musicians and puppets, as well as precious, semi-precious and artificial jewellery. The north-eastern state of Assam offers wicker furniture while West Bengal has *jamdani* and *tangail saris*.

Another popular state-run retail outlet in Connaught Place is the Khadi Gramodyog Bhawan where you can buy hand spun cotton cloth known as *khadi* and readymade garments made from it, besides other items such as handmade paper. *Khadi* was popularised by renowned Indian nationalist Mahatma Gandhi during his lifetime, and to honour the great leader, this store offers a special discount in October every year to commemorate his birth anniversary, which falls on 2 October.

CHANDNI CHOWK

Its name denotes a 'moonlit square' but Chandni Chowk, the main commercial centre and the quintessence of old Delhi, today comes no where near to living up to this definition. However, there was a time, 300 years ago, when it did. That was the heyday of Mughal Emperor Shah Jahan's empire in the 17th century when he created the city of Shahjahanabad to replace Agra as his capital. Chandni Chowk was established by Shah Jahan's favourite daughter Jahanara, as an open octagonal space with an arcade of shops. It was named after a canal, a branch of the Yamuna River, which ran through its centre and shimmered alluringly in the moonlight, hence the name 'chandni' (moonlight).

This commercial 'square' soon expanded in all directions to become a bustling trading centre, with the entire area being commonly referred to as Chandni Chowk. Today, Chandni

LOCATION:

Old Delhi. Closed on Sunday. Nearest Metro Station: Chandni Chowk

Chowk stretches from the Red Fort or Lal Qila at one end, to Fatehpuri Masjid at the other end, with a labyrinth of narrow congested lanes or *galis* in between brimming over with bazaars selling an overwhelming array of goods from car parts to wedding accessories to spices.

Amid the bazaars can be found historic places of worship, with mosques, Hindu and Jain temples and Sikh *gurdwaras* equally well represented. The Jama Masjid, India's largest mosque, is close by. But where there was once a row of banyan trees running down the centre, next to the canal with a platform where people could socialise, today there is a road divider, and a perpetual snarl of traffic. A medley of rickshaws, bicycles and cars blaring their horns has replaced the horse-drawn carriages, palanquins and royal elephants that passed through the street hundreds of years ago.

One of the main attractions of Chandni Chowk is its jewellery market called Dariba Kalan established by Shah Jahan for his trinket-loving daughters. Many of the goldsmiths have moved away, but there are plenty of silver shops to provide interesting buys at competitive prices. Dariba Kalan is also known for *meenakari* or enamelling on gold and silver, engraving of marble and for its perfume shops, notably Gulab Singh Johrimal which has been around since 1816. Its *mithai* or sweetmeat sellers are also a draw. For artificial jewellery, specifically bangles, there is the Churiwali Gali or Bangle Sellers Lane, which has numerous shops selling bangles of all kinds. These wrist adornments come in a variety of materials, colours and designs. Also available are special bangles worn by a new bride.

Chandni Chowk offers much more than just bangles for brides. At glittering Kinari Bazaar, a haven for gold-embellished *sari* and *zardozi* embroidery, there is a profusion of bridal wear and accessories available, including a ready-to-use garland made of *rupees* instead of flowers. And for those on a small budget, there is always the option of hiring bridal ware and accessories from Vishal Chitrashala Dresswala. Outfits for use in theatrical productions can also be obtained here.

For wholesale fabrics, the market to visit is Katra Neel, a knot of cramped stalls named after manufacturers and sellers of the whitening agent *neel* or indigo. The word *katra* refers to an enclosed market. Here you can find an assortment of silks, cottons, as well as the heavier brocade. Katra Neel witnessed unrest during the

There is never a dull moment at Chandni Chowk, a historic market that offers the best bargains.

days of the Sepoy Mutiny in 1857 and the Quit India Movement of the 1900s. A cotton market behind Jama Masjid specialises in quilts, pillows, mattresses and bedding while nearby Meena Bazaar has readymade garments and local cosmetics.

Other notable markets in the area are the second-hand book market at Nai Sarak, a street leading off Chandni Chowk, which is a haven for book lovers looking for cheap buys, specialised school and college books and out-of-print tomes. Nai Sarak leads on to Chawri Bazaar, well known for its copper and brass utensils and paper products available wholesale. Wedding cards and even wallpaper are particularly sought after here. Further down at the Fatehpuri Masjid end of Chandni Chowk is Khari Baoli, which lays claim to being Asia's largest spices and dry fruits market. Here you will encounter mounds of turmeric, coriander and red chillies, sitting side by side with walnuts and almonds stored in jute bags lined up outside the shops.

Then there is Matia Mahal Bazaar, renowned for its traditional Muslim food; Paranthewali Gali, where vendors specialise in mouth-watering *paranthas*, a kind of fried Indian bread stuffed with a variety of fillings, vegetarian or meat; the cycle market with its array of new and old bicycles; the meat market, where you will also find animals designated for slaughter; the fish market; the flower market; and the electronics market at Bhagirath Palace which lays claim to being the largest of its kind in Asia. Bhagirath Palace was originally a mansion belonging to Begum Samru, the colourful widow of a European mercenary officer.

Chandni Chowk is known for its commercial establishments but the area is also a valuable showcase of historic buildings, particularly places of worship belonging to different faiths, exemplifying the area's enduring tradition of religious harmony.

Besides Chandni Chowk's once magnificent courtyard houses or *havelis*, many of which are crumbling and in need of repair, or have been converted into shops and offices, there are a number of notable buildings with an interesting past. These include the Town Hall, the Office of the Municipal Commissioner of Delhi built in 1860 to 1864 and the State Bank of India Building, set up in 1861 as the Delhi and London Bank.

The Digamber Jain Lal Mandir is said to be the oldest temple of the Jain community in the city, having been built in 1526 and enlarged in the 1870s. It has a charity bird hospital attached to

Mounds of spices lined up in the open are a common sight in Khari Baoli, said to be Asia's largest spice and dry fruit market.

it. Among other places places of worship are the Gurudwara Sis Ganj constructed in the memory of ninth Sikh Guru Tegh Bahadur who was beheaded at the orders of Mughal Emperor Aurangzeb at the Kotwali police station at this site in November 1675; Fatehpuri Masjid built in 1650 and named after Fatehpuri Begum, one of Shah Jaha's wives. In the 19th century, public debates between Muslim and Christian religious leaders were held here; Sunehri Masjid, an 18th century mosque with three gilded copper domes; and Gauri-Shankar temple, dating back to the 18th century and believed to hold an 800-year-old *linga*, the symbol of Hindu God Shiva.

CONNAUGHT PLACE

A sprawling commercial centre in the heart of Delhi, Connaught Place is distinguished by its singular concentric design and its colonnaded buildings with high-ceilinged verandahs harking back to the British colonial era. It was built in 1933 by the Public Works Department, with the head of its architects department, Robert Tor Russell, overseeing the project. Interestingly, Connaught Place was named after British King George V's uncle, the Duke of Connaught, who visited Delhi in 1921 at the planning stage of this grand shopping centre designed for the British and Indian elite.

In 1995, the Indian government renamed it Rajiv Chowk (Rajiv Circle) after the late Prime Minister Rajiv Gandhi. The outer circle of Connaught Place, known as Connaught Circus was renamed Indira Chowk (Indira Circle) after the late Indira Gandhi, a former prime minister and Rajiv Gandhi's mother. But despite its renaming, this commercial nucleus is still popularly known by the name given to it by the British, Connaught Place or CP for short.

A key part of chief British architect Edwin Landseer Lutyens' master plan for the British imperial capital New Delhi, Connaught Place has eight roads radiating from it, with only one-way traffic permitted for a smooth flow. In the middle of this circular design is a central park below which is the underground metro station on one side, and the bustling air-conditioned market Palika Bazaar on the other side. Neither the metro station nor Palika Bazaar was part of the original Connaught Place, which comprised the inner and outer circles.

In the years since 1947 when the British left India, Connaught Place has expanded in all directions to include surrounding shopping areas on major roads such as Janpath and Baba Kharak Singh Marg. Today it is home to all kinds of commercial and retail establishments from toy and sports stores to boutiques, bookshops, jewellery outlets, travel agents, airline offices, banks, hotels and guest houses, homegrown handicraft and handloom emporiums and bakeries, fast food eateries and restaurants offering a variety of cuisines.

Some of the noteworthy outlets are Mehrasons for jewellery, Hidesign for leather bags, Planet M and Music World for music,

At the centre of circular Connaught Place lies Central Park where shoppers can take a breather after a hectic day out.

LOCATION:
Central Delhi.
Closed on Sunday.
Nearest Metro
Station: Rajiv
Chowk

Mohanlal Sons and Snowhite for readymade garments, Nalli for *saris*, The Bookworm for books, and Dev Crockery Store for household items. Some of the preferred eateries and restaurants are Berco's for Chinese cuisine, Nirula's for Indian fast food, Rodeo for Tex-Mex cuisine and The Embassy for Indian and multi-cuisine fare. Wenger's pastry shop, which pioneered Swiss confectionery in Delhi, has been providing residents with sumptuous patties, pastries and other bakery items since 1926.

The commercial outlets stand side by side in the circular arcades, displaying their wares in colourful show windows. Shoppers can stroll comfortably along the covered verandahs of the inner circle, divided into six blocks running from A to F, and separated by the eight radial roads. The outer circle has blocks G to P. Cheap wares such as new and second-hand books, artificial jewellery, bags, wall hangings and trinkets are also sold by hawkers and pavement stalls at bargain prices throughout Connaught Place.

Janpath is a major thoroughfare that connects Connaught Place to the south end of what was British New Delhi. In those days the road was called Queensway. Janpath, literally meaning 'road of the people', is famous for its colourful market, particularly

With offices and retail outlets drawing the crowds, it can be a challenge to find a parking spot if you drive, although there are designated parking areas for motorcycles.

the Tibetan stalls where you can get all kinds of handicrafts and jewellery in stone, metal, bone and wood at reasonable prices. Bargaining is the norm in Janpath stores where trendy made-in-India clothes and fashion accessories are available in plenty and at reasonable prices, as are Rajasthani paintings and brassware. Janpath is also well known for the Central Cottage Industries Emporium (see page 28), a storehouse of Indian crafts and textiles popular with both locals and tourists, and the exclusive jewellery showroom Tribhuvandas Bhimji Zhaveri.

During the days of the British and for many years after independence in 1947, Connaught Place was the primary commercial centre in the city, attracting people from far-flung areas for day-long shopping excursions or just to spend a day out with the family and friends. Over the years, following Delhi's monumental growth, markets have sprung up in all the major sections of the city such as South Extension, Ajmal Khan Road, Lajpat Nagar and Greater Kailash, so people need no longer travel long distances to come to Connaught Place. However, for tourists visiting the Indian capital, a trip to bustling Connaught Place is definitely a must, if only to catch a glimpse of the one-time 'queen' of Delhi's retail establishment.

CRAFTS

Craftsmen have thrived in Delhi since the days of the Mughal rulers. In those early days when Shahjahanabad, now old Delhi, was the centre of activity, silver and gold enamelling known as *meenakari*, ivory carving and gold thread embroidery called *zari* and *zardozi* were among the most sought after trades. Except for ivory which has now been banned, the crafts tradition continues to this day with thousands of workshops thriving in the commercial maze of old Delhi just like they did hundreds of years ago. The city also has expert potters who specialise in terracotta and blue pottery. Then there are wooden toy and kite makers, and craftsmen who create colourful bangles made of the hardened resin lac.

Enamelling or Meenakari

Silver and gold enamelling came to India with the Mughals in the 16th century. The process involves fusing different mineral substances on metal to produce a colourful glaze in a variety of designs. The craftsman draws the design on the metal creating grooves, which are then filled with enamel dust. The metal is then fired in a furnace where the coloured enamel melts and spreads evenly in the groove. The colours, the most popular being red, green and white, are fired one by one, with white being the most heat resistant applied first. Gold is preferred for *meenakari* because of the wide range of colours that can be applied to it.

Ivory Carving

This ancient Indian craft was once popular in the southern cities of Trivandrum, Bangalore and Mysore, besides Delhi, Varanasi, Jaipur and Jodhpur and Amritsar in the north. Ivory, taken from elephant tusks, was carved into decorative items like boxes, plates and jewellery. In Delhi, floral motifs, geometrical patterns and fine latticework were popular. Today, instead of ivory, many carvers now use ivory chips and bone with excellent results.

Zari and Zardozi

Originally created by Muslim craftsmen for nobles in the Mughal empire, *zari* and its more elaborate version known as *zardozi* are gold threads embroidered into fabrics to create glittering Indian outfits as well as more contemporary fusion wear. Instead of real gold, which was used traditionally to adorn the fabrics, today what is applied is synthetic *zari* embroidery. To create synthetic *zari*, ingots of metal are melted and pressed through steel sheets to make thin wires and other adornments such as spangles and dots. *Zardozi* involves embroidery with a combination of gold threads, spangles, beads and seed pearls on silk, satin or velvet. Traditional patterns include florals, but geometric designs have been incorporated into this age-old needlework craft.

Pottery

Delhi was once known for its blue clay pottery. In this style, powdered quartz and gum are mixed together to make a semi-transparent soft paste which is then moulded into shape before the object is glazed and fired. Items such as ashtrays, vases, coasters, bowls and boxes are created in blue, and sometimes combined with green, for a colourful finish. Hazarilal, who has carried on the blue pottery tradition of his forbears in old Delhi, is one of the few remaining practitioners of this trade today. Delhi is also known for its terracotta pottery, with designs being both decorative and utilitarian.

Gold is the popular choice for *meenakari* work, brought to India by the Mughals in the 16th century.

CRICKET

The favourite game of Indians and the unofficial national sport, the origins of cricket in India can be traced back to the British in the 18th century. It was British sailors on shore leave who first played a cricket match on Indian soil in 1721. Later the Parsi community in Mumbai became actively involved in it and formed the Oriental Cricket Club, the first of its kind in the country.

Cricket in India received official recognition with the formation of the Board of Control for Cricket in India (BCCI) in 1929 which was followed three years later, on 25 June 1932, by India's first test match, played against the British team at Lord's, England. The Indian team lost despite commendable

LOCATION:
Bahadur Shah
Zafar Marg. Nearest
Metro Station:
Pragati Maidan.

Cricket came to
Delhi with the
British, and is now
the most popular
sport, played in
neighbourhood
gardens and at
the Firoz Shah
Kotla Stadium.

performances by its pacemen Mohammad Nissar, Amar Singh and Jahangir Khan.

Since then cricket has become a national passion with fans avidly playing the sport at clubs and even neighbourhood parks while closely following the progress of India's players in international matches and the domestic arena where teams compete for the Ranji Trophy, Irani Trophy and the Duleep Trophy. Delhi, like other Indian cities, is engulfed in cricket fever when any major international or national championship is underway, particularly if it is being played at the city's Firoz Shah Kotla Stadium.

Firoz Shah Kotla, established in 1883 and named after Firoz Shah Tughlaq, the third monarch of the Tughlaq Dynasty who ruled the Delhi Sultanate from 1351 to 1388, is rated among the top four cricket venues in the country. The stadium is located on Bahadur Shah Zafar Marg Road and is owned by the Delhi District Cricket Association. It was at Firoz Shah Kotla that India hosted its first test match after independence from the British in 1947. The match against the West Indies led by John Goddard, was held from 10 to 14 November 1948 and ended in a draw.

The stadium has also been witness to a number of cricket feats. In 1952, during India's test match against Pakistan, batsmen Hemu Adhikari and Ghulam Ahmed were involved in a record tenth wicket stand of 109 runs, while in 1965, off spinner S Venkataraghavan tore apart the New Zealand batsmen, achieving 8 for 72 and 4 for 80. In 1983 to 1984, batsman Sunil Gavaskar, nicknamed the 'Little Master', achieved his 29th century at Firoz Shah Kotla, a record which equalled cricket legend Don Bradman's for the highest number of hundreds in test matches. But Firoz Shah Kotla's most significant milestone was leg spinner Anil Kumble's haul of ten wickets for 74 runs against Pakistan in 1999.

Located near the Firoz Shah Kotla cricket stadium are the crumbling ruins of the Firoz Shah Kotla Fort that stood at the heart of Firozabad, the city built by Firoz Shah Tughlaq in 1354, and generally referred to as the fifth city of Delhi. A 12.8-metre high Ashoka Pillar installed here by Firoz Shah, dating back to the days of Emperor Ashoka (r. 273-232 BC), who inscribed his edicts on pillars, still stands today among the remains of this once massive citadel.

CULTURAL **CAPITAL**

A cultural epicentre during the heyday of the Delhi Sultanate and the Mughal empire in medieval India, Delhi remains a focal point for dance, music and other performing arts even in the present day. The city's cultural calendar is busy round the year, except for a lull during the scorching summer months. Activity picks up again by August, gathering momentum during winter until it tapers off by the end of April. The city offers major annual cultural events as well as smaller dance and music recitals and plays organised by highly talented local and foreign artistes.

With music festivals, dance dramas and theatre performances, Delhi's cultural calendar is busy all year round.

Delhi's cultural hub lies in an area known informally as Mandi House after the headquarters of the state-owned television network Doordarshan located on Copernicus Marg (Road). Clustered around a green landscaped roundabout, a couple of kilometres away from Connaught Place and adjacent to Bengali Market, are such prominent establishments as Rabindra Bhawan, the headquarters of the Lalit Kala Akademi (Academy of Fine Arts), the Sahitya Natak Akademi (Academy of Music and Dance) and Sahitya Akademi (Academy of Literature); Bhawalpur House, where the premier National School of Drama and the Kathak Kendra Dance Academy are located; Triveni Kala Sangam, which has exhibition galleries and an open air theatre; Shri Ram Centre for Performing Arts, and Kamani Auditorium, both popular venues for staging plays, dance performances and concerts. Internationally renowned Indian dancers such as Yamini Krishnamurty, Raja and Radha Reddy, Uma Sharma and Birju Maharaj have their schools in Delhi.

Delhi's cultural calendar begins in January with the week-long Republic Day Folk Dance Festival, which brings together performers from regional states in a colourful display of talent. This festival is held at the Talkatora Indoor Stadium and other venues in the city, and runs until 29 January, the last day of the Republic Day festivities. Talkatora is also the venue for the annual Garden Tourism Festival held in February, and the Mango Festival in July. During both events, a multitude of theme-based cultural performances are staged for visitors. In March comes the eagerly anticipated Shriram Shankarlal Music Festival, a celebration of classical music which brings together such notables as vocalists Rashid Khan and Sulochana Brahaspati, and flute exponent Hari Prasad Chaurasia on a single platform. In the summer months, the National School of Drama holds its annual Summer Theatre Festival organised by its repertory company.

Come October and the 13th century Qutb Minar tower is the magnificent backdrop of the Qutb Festival of Classical Music and Dance scheduled during the full moon period. This three-day cultural feast celebrates Delhi's heritage with a series of dance and music recitals by notable artists such as classical dancer Sonal Mansingh, classical singer Ustaad Ahmad Hussain and musician Bhajan Sopori. The performances are held in the evenings on the

grounds surrounding the Qutb Minar with the spectators seated comfortably on the grass. Food stalls offering specialties from different corners of India add to the charm of this event.

There is never a dull moment as streetside musicians add to the festivities.

October is also the month when the Hindu festival of Dussehra is celebrated with the Ram Leela dance dramas, during which the story of Lord Rama and demon king Ravana as told in the Hindu epic *Ramayana*, is enacted. The month of dance dramas ends in a display of fireworks on Dussehra day when effigies of Ravana, his brother Kumbhakaran and son Meghnad, are set ablaze to commemorate the victory of good over evil. Ananya—the Purana Qila Dance Festival also takes place in October, amid the ruins of the 16th century Purana Qila or Old Fort. It features classical Indian dance forms like Kathak, Odissi, Kuchipudi, Mohiniattam and Bharatnatyam presented by such eminent performers as Raja and Radha Reddy and Neena Prasad.

DELHI **ATTIRE**

The Indian capital represents a fascinating amalgam of styles and traditions drawn from different regions when it comes to the clothes its residents wear. This metropolis is a virtual microcosm of clothing trends prevalent across the country. While traditional attire is generally favoured by older women, the younger set prefers Western contemporary clothing such as jeans, skirts, tops and t-shirts. Indian men in Delhi are commonly dressed in a pant and shirt or suits for more formal wear, opting for ethnic attire only during religious functions, weddings and festivals. Traditional attire for women includes the *sari*, *salwar kameez*, *churidar kurta* and *lehenga* while for men it is the *dhoti kurta*, *sherwani* and *kurta* pyjama. Fabrics vary with the seasons, with cool chiffon, georgette, cotton and handloom weaves preferred in summer when temperatures can cross 45°C, while in winter, the warmer silk, velvet, brocade and polyester are favoured.

Sari

The *sari*, which derives its name from the Sanskrit word meaning cloth, can be traced back to the ancient Indus Valley Civilisation. A simple piece of unstitched cloth draped around the body has evolved into a six yard long stitched drape worn with a blouse and an underskirt. The *sari*, as worn in Delhi, is commonly tied around the waist, with pleats tucked into the petticoat at the front and the end or *pallav* draped across the chest to fall over one shoulder. The design, style and weave of the *sari* differs from region to region, with the south especially acclaimed for its exquisite *Kancheevaram* silks while the north is renowned for its *tanchois* among others. In the western state of Maharashtra, the traditional *sari* is nine yards in length and worn drawn between the legs for ease of movement. Delhi has a potpourri of *sari* styles representative of the diverse communities that live within its geographical boundaries.

Salwar kameez/Churidar kurta

The *salwar kameez* is an ensemble of long, form-fitting tunic and baggy drawstring pyjamas accompanied by a long scarf or *dupatta* that has its origins in the Mughal period of Indian history. This traditional attire was later popularised by Punjabis and is now worn throughout India. The *churidar* is a tight fitting pant with

On the streets of
Delhi, you can see
ladies in a variety of
attire including the
sari and the *salwar
kameez*.

churis or bangle-like folds around the ankles. It is accompanied by a long and loose tunic called a *kurta*. Both the *kurta* and *kameez* are similar in design and worn interchangeably. They vary in length depending on the prevailing fashion trends. A variation of this attire is the *kurta* pyjama worn by men.

Lehnga choli

The *lehnga* is a long flowing skirt worn with a tight-fitting blouse or *choli* which leaves the midriff bare, accompanied by a long scarf or *dupatta*. The *lehnga*, daily wear in the states of Rajasthan and Gujarat, is popular attire in Delhi for special occasions such as festivals and weddings. It is preferred by brides who usually opt for brighter hues like red or maroon and intricate gold thread embroidery.

Dhoti kurta

The *dhoti kurta* is a traditional *lungi*-type garment worn by men. The *dhoti* is a rectangular piece of unstitched cloth, around five yards long, wrapped around the midriff and tucked between the legs. It is commonly worn with a loose long tunic. A *dhoti*, made of homespun *khadi* cotton cloth, was the garment favoured by Mahatma Gandhi after he abandoned his western attire of pants and shirt. Gandhi usually wore a simple shawl with his *dhoti*.

Sherwani

A long coat-like garment with a high collar worn with tight pants or *churidar* pyjama, and may be accompanied by a shawl. This ensemble, which has its origins in the days of the Muslim dynasties who established the Delhi Sultanate (1206-1526), is commonly worn by bridegrooms.

DELHI GOLF CLUB

The British introduced golf to India and in 1931 established Delhi's first golf course, the Delhi Golf Club, originally known as the Lodhi Golf Course. With its verdant trees and shrubs, and historic monuments dating back to the period when the Lodhi Dynasty ruled the Delhi Sultanate in the 15th to 16th centuries, the Delhi Golf Club provides a different golfing experience compared to conventional courses. The 6,972 yards, par-72, 18-hole course located on Dr Zakir Husain Marg Road, near Oberoi Hotel, also abounds with over 300 species of birds. It is not unusual to see peacocks on the rolling greens of this club which has a 9-hole Peacock Course named after these stunning birds. The oldest golf course in the city was redesigned in 1977 by Australian golfer Peter Thompson.

Since the early days, the course has grown to become one of the most prestigious sporting venues in India. It hosted the first ever golf tournament of the Asian Games in 1982 as well as the Indian Open, part of the Asian PGA circuit. In February 2008, it hosted the US$2.5 million Indian Masters tournament, the first European Tour-sanctioned golfing event to be held in India and also the richest golfing event in the country.

LOCATION:
Dr Zakir Hussain Marg Road, south Delhi
Tel: 24365105/ 24362235

♡ DELHI **METRO**

The Delhi Metro, only the second subway in the country after Kolkata, is the new pride of the Indian capital. It was as recently as October 1998 that construction on Delhi's subway, desperately needed in a city with an overburdened public transport system, began in earnest after years of planning. Four years later, by 25 December 2002, commercial operations for the first section, between Shahdara and Tis Hazari in the north east, had begun and the Metro's air-conditioned coaches were ferrying passengers.

Since those early days, a total of three lines running across the city and linking Shahdara to Rithala, Vishwa Vidhyala to Central Secretariat and Indrapratha to Dwarka, are under operation bringing the total length of the Metro to 65.1 km with as many as 59 underground, elevated and at grade stations. Phase 2 of the project is underway and will add 100 km of track to the network and is expected to be completed by 2010, in time for the Commonwealth Games to be held in Delhi.

The building of the Delhi Metro on schedule and within budget has earned the Delhi Metro Rail Corporation Ltd (DMRC) and its managing director Elattuvalapil Sreedharan, high praise from all quarters. The feat is particularly remarkable when compared to the experience in Kolkata, where it took 23 years to build 20 km of the subway at a cost 12 times more than the allocated budget.

The Delhi Metro has not only brought with it greater mobility but a completely automated fare collection system which is the first of its kind in the city. Passengers can opt for single journey tokens or stored value commuter cards depending on their requirements and frequency of travel. There is a special tourist card, valid for one to three days, suitable for short-term visitors to Delhi. Trains run from 6am to 11pm with the frequency ranging from four minutes to 12 minutes depending on peak and non-peak hours of travel. Passengers can use feeder buses, autorickshaws or taxis for their outward journey from the metro stations.

DELHI UNIVERSITY

Delhi University is not only an august institution of learning, but also the site of 19th and early 20th century buildings of the British Raj. These buildings, in the north Delhi campus of the University, stand testimony to the significant role the area played when the British first moved into Delhi, before Edwin Lutyens created the new imperial capital (see Lutyen's New Delhi, page 88).

In 1922, Delhi's first university started with three colleges, two faculties and a cohort of 750 students in the Civil Lines area. Since those early days, Delhi University has literally grown in all directions, having established colleges in other parts of the city to cope with the large number of students. Today it is among Asia's largest premier institutions with two active campuses and two more on the way, 14 faculties, 86 academic departments, 79 colleges and a student body of 220,000 students.

The university began its expansion drive in the 1970s, when it shifted some of its postgraduate programmes to a rented building in south Delhi. This developed into a full-fledged second campus in the 1980s and now the university is looking to set up more campuses in east and west Delhi for its medical and engineering faculties respectively. However, the hub of the

The lofty hallways of Delhi's oldest university speak of a bygone era.

university remains in north Delhi, where its oldest colleges, St Stephen's, Hindu and Ramjas are located, along with the university offices, housed in the Viceregal Lodge Estate. The Viceregal House, a long low building which now serves as the office of the Vice Chancellor, was once known as Circuit House, the official guest house for British officers. The last Viceroy of British India, Lord Mountbatten, proposed to his wife Edwina in a room in this historic building.

St Stephen's, Delhi University's oldest college, is a red brick building designed by architect Walter George who also planned the Faculty of Arts and Miranda House, a leading women's college in the campus. St Stephen's, founded in 1881 by a Christian mission from Westcott House, Cambridge, United Kingdom, moved here from its original premises on Zorawar Singh Marg in the Kashmere Gate area. That stately building, with arched colonnades and a domed pavilion, was designed by Samuel Swinton Jacob and is presently being used by the Election Commission of Delhi.

LOCATION:

North campus
is located in
Civil Lines
Tel: 27667725;
South Campus is on
Benito Juarez Marg,
near Dhaula Kuan,
south Delhi
Tel: 24110759/
24114634.
Nearest Metro
Station to
North Campus:
Vishwavidyalaya
Website:
http://www.du.ac.in

Indraprastha College for Women, the first women's college in the university, is another remarkable building from the British era. The building, named Alipur House, was originally the office of the British commander-in-chief in India. Set amid green lawns and royal palm trees, it is a single-storeyed red and yellow building with a distinctive façade of semi-circular arches. Indraprastha College, which has been brought up to date with the addition of computer labs and an audiovisual centre, has been earmarked as a heritage building by the Indian government.

Other symbols of British colonial rule in and around the vast north Delhi campus and its adjoining scrub-covered outcrop called the Ridge, include the Old Secretariat building, Metcalf House and Mutiny Memorial. The oldest of these is Metcalf House which was built by Sir Thomas Metcalf, a commissioner of Delhi from 1835 to 1853 who died after being poisoned. The mansion, built in the 1830s, suffered extensive damage during the Sepoy Mutiny of 1857 and was rebuilt in 1913. Metcalf House is owned by the government and is used as its Defence Services Documentation Centre. Close to Metcalf House is the Old Secretariat built in 1912 as the office of the government secretariat. It is now occupied by the Delhi government. Mutiny Memorial, a tapering octagonal-shaped sandstone tower, was built in 1863 by the British to honour soldiers killed during the Sepoy Mutiny of 1857. Their names are engraved on stone slabs around the tower. Another British-era building in the area is the Residency, the official house of the Resident of the British East India Company. This was originally a Mughal building, known as Dara Shikoh's Library after Shah Jahan's favourite son Dara Shikoh, before the British took it over.

DILLI **HAAT**

The weekly village market or *haat*, common throughout rural India, has found a permanent home in Delhi. The state-owned Dilli Haat, located in south Delhi and run by the Delhi Tourism Corporation, brings together craftsmen from around the country to sell their handicrafts in a stone and brick rural setting reminiscent of a village market. This open-air crafts paradise, which also offers a variety of food stalls from different states, came into being in March 1994 as a show window of the best of Indian art and culture. It was also designed to encourage needy craftsmen and provide them with a low-cost retail outlet where they could sell directly to customers.

Open throughout the year, Dilli Haat occupies a prime green 2.4-hectare area near the All India Institute of Medical Sciences and INA market. It comprises a plaza with stalls and kiosks made of brick, stone and thatched roofs and courtyards with trees and shrubs, creating the perfect ambience for a rural bazaar. The stalls sell everything from textiles, ready-to-wear ethnic outfits, puppets, dolls, pottery, brass, cane and bamboo, footwear as well as sandalwood carvings and jewellery. There are 62 fixed stalls which are leased out for 15 days at a time on a rotational basis to

An open-air crafts paradise where shoppers can buy handicrafts from the artisans themselves.

provide variety to visitors. However, the number of stalls varies depending on the season and tourist arrivals, with the number going up to 200 and more in the peak winter season. Craftsmen sit in these stalls and display their wares on stone platforms. In some stalls, visitors can see the craftsmen at work, skilfully creating a piece of costume jewellery or a puppet.

Prices are usually moderate and negotiable, and most goods are priced lower than what they would be available for at the state emporiums in Connaught Place. However, quality may vary from craftsman to craftsman since it is not controlled by the government. There is a small state-run souvenir shop on the premises where prices are fixed and quality is assured.

Besides the crafts stalls, there are about 25 food stalls serving popular dishes from different states such as *momos* (a type of dumpling) from Sikkim, bamboo chicken from Nagaland, *dosa* (a type of crepe) and the steamed rice cake *idli* from the southern states and *dhokla* (a savoury made from gram flour) from Gujarat. Dilli Haat also holds cultural programmes representative of different states from time to time, to showcase India's rich cultural heritage.

DIPLOMATIC ENCLAVE CHANAKYAPURI

With its broad tree-lined avenues, wide open spaces and palatial buildings, Chanakyapuri lives up to its image as Delhi's upscale diplomatic enclave. Located in the central zone of south Delhi, about 7 km from Connaught Place, Chanakyapuri presents a welcome change from the clustered environs of the other residential colonies of the Indian capital. Embassies and international schools abound here making it a self-contained enclave for the city's diplomats and expatriate community.

Running from north to south through the centre of Chanakyapuri is Shanti Path (literally the 'path of peace'), the main artery of this colony and where many of Delhi's foreign missions are located. These include the United States, the United Kingdom, Russia, Canada, France, Japan, Germany, Australia, the Netherlands, China, Pakistan and Afghanistan.

The US embassy, dating back to 1959, is noteworthy for its elaborate design blending Eastern and Western concepts. It was created by architect Edward Durrell Stone, who also designed the Kennedy Centre for the Performing Arts in Washington DC. The complex occupies a 11.3 hectare site and holds the chancery, the residence of the ambassador known as Roosevelt House, offices and accommodation for embassy officials. The Belgian

Chanakyapuri is a posh self-contained colony where many of Delhi's foreign missions are located.

Gyarah Murti (meaning 11 statues, the number that makes up the sculpture) was created by Bengali sculptor Devi Prasad Roy Choudhary.

embassy, created by prominent Indian artist Satish Gujral, is a unique blend of modern and traditional Indian architectural elements. The American, British and German schools are also located in Chanakyapuri, while the Japanese school is located nearby in Vasant Vihar.

Besides foreign missions, Chanakyapuri has a number of luxury hotels such as the state-owned Ashoka and Samrat, and the Maurya Sheraton and Taj Palace. These hotels are popular among Delhi residents for their specialty restaurants such as the Bukhara at the Maurya Sheraton and the Frontier at the Ashoka.

Linking Chankyapuri to the rest of the city is the busy Sardar Patel Marg, named after prominent freedom fighter Sardar Vallabhbhai Patel who was the first Home Minister and Deputy Prime Minister in independent India. Situated at the junction of Sardar Patel Marg and Willingdon Crescent is an imposing sculpture of Mahatma Gandhi and his followers undertaking the famous Salt March in March to April 1930 to protest against the harsh salt taxes imposed by the British. The bronze sculpture, known as *Gyarah Murti* depicts the father of the nation, dressed in his trademark attire of loin cloth and shawl, and carrying a staff in his right hand, leading other nationalists to the coastal town of Dandi from Ahmedabad in Gujarat state. The procession reached Dandi on 6 April after walking for 23 days. At the seashore in Dandi, Gandhi picked up a lump of mud and salt and boiled it to create salt in defiance of the existing law.

LOCATION:
South Delhi, about 7km from Connaught Place.

GURGAON AND NOISE

A metropolis with an accruing migrant population, Delhi has had to extend its boundaries to include its suburbs, Gurgaon and Noida, under the all-encompassing National Capital Region (NCR). These two satellite towns, Gurgaon to the south of Delhi and Noida towards the east, have grown rapidly to become upscale residential areas and commercial hubs for Delhi residents. Condominiums, bungalows with landscaped gardens, farmhouses, golf clubs, theme parks, corporate offices, shopping malls, schools, higher educational institutes and healthcare facilities have mushroomed in Gurgaon and Noida, with developers preferring to build in these areas as real estate rates spiral in overpopulated and congested Delhi.

Dubbed the Millennium City, Gurgaon was once 'Guru-gram', a village that existed in the time of the Pandava brothers in the Hindu epic *Mahabharata*. According to legend, the Pandavas presented Guru-gram to their teacher Dronacharya to express their appreciation for his efforts. Today, Gurgaon has grown into an important centre for multinationals such as GE, Microsoft, IBM, Oracle, Nokia, and American Express as well as local companies involved in everything from software to web services to haute couture.

Gurgaon has become the choice destination for companies keen to start operations in Delhi. Its modern glass and chrome office complexes are juxtaposed with swank condominiums offering residents full club facilities and the all-important power back-up to run their air-conditioners and heaters during extreme seasonal temperatures. And, at a stone's throw away are well-equipped shopping malls such as MGF Metropolitan Mall, Sahara Mall, DT Mega Mall and Gold Souk where top international retailers have set up shop along with popular Indian stores such as Shopper's Stop, Landmark and Westside.

Noida stands for the New Okhla Industrial Development Authority which was established in 1976 as an integrated industrial township in the state of Uttar Pradesh. Today, it is a thriving commercial, industrial, educational and media centre in the National Capital Region, home to the Noida Software Technology Park (STP), Noida Export Processing Zone (NEPZ), the Noida Film City, institutions such as Amity

LOCATION:

Gurgaon, to the south of Delhi. Website: http://gurgaon.nic.in/

Noida, to the east of Delhi. Website: http://www.noidaauthorityonline.com/

Business School and the Infosys Computer Education Centre, and popular shopping malls like Centre Stage Mall, Spice World and the Unitech mall at Great India Place.

The Film City, established in 1988, is a 40.5 hectare landscaped complex that has become a nucleus for film and television production and media training, having the premier Asian Academy of Film & Television (AAFT) and more than a dozen studios belonging to such celebrated Bollywood producers as Yash Chopra, Boney Kapoor and Sandeep Marwah, on its premises. Television serials, news shows, regional language films as well as acclaimed Bollywood films such as Shekhar Kapur's *Bandit Queen* and Mani Ratnam's *Dil Se* have been shot at Film City, which has impressive outdoor locales on the banks of the Yamuna River. AAFT, strategically located near the studios, lays claim to being the strongest media training centre in Asia. It has trained thousands of students from India and overseas in the intricacies of film and television production, providing students with a unique opportunity to learn on the sets, and from personal encounters with visiting media personalities.

Modern office complexes, condominiums and malls have sprung up in Gurgaon and Noida because of a lack of space in congested Delhi.

HAUZ KHAS **VILLAGE**

These remnants of the 13th and 14th centuries lend a historic charm to the south Delhi colony of Hauz Khas.

A unique shopping experience is available at Hauz Khas Village, an urban village which has been transformed into a trendy and upmarket retail destination. With its mud and brick structures and unpaved lanes where cows and stray dogs roam freely, it lives up to its rustic image even though it has been described as fake by some people. But enter any of the boutiques and art galleries located there and you are transported back to urban Delhi.

Besides its boutiques selling designer *saris*, *salwar kameez* and Western outfits, are handicraft and furniture stores. The art galleries offer works from some of India's pre-eminent painters such as Maqbool Fida Husain. Visitors make their way through cow dung-strewn lanes and dark alleys to reach the stores where prices are high but bargaining is possible. Hauz Khas Village also has some popular restaurants such as Park Baluchi.

This urban village is set within the larger neighbourhood of Hauz Khas, where once Delhi's second historic city Siri was located. Alauddin Khilji of the Khilji dynasty, who ruled Delhi from 1296 to 1316, excavated a large tank in Hauz Khas, then known as Hauz-i-Alai. Firoz Shah Tughlaq (r.1351-88) of the Tughlaq dynasty which succeeded the Khilji dynasty, re-excavated the tank in the 14th century and developed the area by constructing buildings on its south-eastern banks. The area came to be known as Hauz Khas, literally 'royal tank'. The tank which once covered an area of 50 hectares, is smaller today, and remains dry for most of the year. Part of it has been converted into a garden which is popular with joggers.

Firoz Shah, who was passionate about buildings, constructed his own tomb of local quartzite rubble and sandstone in Hauz Khas, along with an Islamic theological school or *madrasa*. The double-storey *madrasa* was famous for its Islamic teachings as well as its architectural design, particularly its balconies overlooking the tank. The tomb adjoins the *madrasa* and actually connects its two wings. These historic buildings are within a walled enclosure at the end of Hauz Khas Village. Ten years after Firoz Shah's death in 1388, Mongol invader Timur entered Delhi and chose to camp with his men at Hauz Khas. He succeeded in capturing the city.

LOCATION:
Off Aurobindo Marg, south Delhi

HUMAYUN'S TOMB

The precursor of the famous tomb gardens built by the Mughals in India, Humayun's Tomb is a regal edifice built for love just like the famous Taj Mahal in Agra which it inspired. This monument, located on Mathura Road, about 4 km south-east of Connaught Place, is a significant example of early Mughal architecture and occupies a vital place in the history of Delhi.

While the Taj Mahal was Mughal Emperor Shah Jahan's memorial to his late wife Mumtaz Mahal, the tomb of the second Mughal Emperor Humayun was built by his grieving widow Hamida Banu Begum or Haji Begum, with construction beginning almost nine years after his death and completed in 1571.

LOCATION:

Mathura Road, near the crossing with Lodhi Road. Nearest Metro Station: Pragati Maidan.

Haji Begum, the senior wife of Humayun and the mother of his successor Akbar, spent 1.5 million rupees to build the mausoleum which was designed by Persian architect Mirak Mirza Ghiyath. Humayun, who succeeded his father Babur to the throne in 1535, had a short reign, being ousted from power by Afghan Sher Shah in 1540. He returned from exile in 1555 but after six months, fell down the stairs to his death in his library at his palace in the Purana Qila. During the Sepoy Mutiny of 1857, Humayun's Tomb was used as a place of refuge by Bahadur Shah ll, the last Mughal emperor who was merely a figurehead, with the real power being vested in the British.

The red sandstone and marble tomb is a World Heritage property extolled for its structural design and workmanship, a fusion of Persian and Indian architecture. It lacks the elaborate ornamentation and intricate detail of the Taj Mahal, built more than 60 years later, but scores in its exterior proportions and aesthetic design, such as its double dome, which were highly innovative for that time. The tomb itself stands on a platform that is 8 metres high, and has 17 arched openings. Entry into the tomb is through two grand arched double-storey gateways located on the west and south.

Humayun's plain white marble cenotaph lies in the octagonal central chamber.

Inside, surrounded by arched alcoves, is the octagonal central chamber where Humayun's plain white marble cenotaph lies. Many of Humayun's family members, including Haji Begum, lie buried in the adjoining chambers. The building is crowned by a double dome made of sandstone and marble which is bounded by *chhatris* or decorative canopies, one of several Hindu design features in the mausoleum. Decorative lattice screens called *jalis* and *chajjas* or broad eaves, are other Hindu elements incorporated in the design of the building.

The mausoleum is set in an extensive garden called *char bagh*, which literally means four gardens to describe its unique four-square design. The *char bagh*, enclosed by high walls, is divided into four main squares, which are further sub-divided by narrow water channels and raised walkways in an intricate grid pattern. The garden has undergone extensive restoration work carried out by the Archaeological Survey of India and the Aga Khan Foundation.

Standing close to Humayun's Tomb are several other buildings of historic interest. These include Arab ki Sarai, an enclosure constructed to house 300 Arabs whom Haji Begum brought with her to Delhi after her pilgrimage to Mecca; Afsarwala Tomb and Mosque, within Arab ki Sarai; the Tomb of Isa Khan, a nobleman in Sher Shah's court; Bu Halima's Garden; Nila Gumbad or Blue Dome; and Nai ka Gumbad or Barber's Tomb.

INDIA GATE AND
THE AMAR JAWAN JYOTI

Standing at a crossroads in central Delhi, on the eastern end of Rajpath (formerly Kingsway) is India Gate. Originally called the All India War Memorial, it salutes the 70,000 Indian soldiers killed in World War I and the 13,516 British and Indian soldiers who died in the 1919 Afghan War.

India Gate was designed by Edwin Lutyens, the chief architect of British New Delhi, and its foundation stone was laid by the Duke of Connaught in 1921. However, it was dedicated to the nation only 10 years later in 1931 by then Viceroy Lord Irwin. The mammoth structure has a red stone base and a cornice inscribed with the imperial suns on top. Above the cornice are a series of steps which end in a circular bowl that was designed to contain burning oil to sustain a blazing fire on important occasions. The word India is written on both sides of the arch, accompanied by the date MCMXIV (1914) on the left and MCMXIX (1919) on the right in memory of the soldiers killed in the two wars.

Years later, on 26 January 1972, the Amar Jawan Jyoti (literally flame of the immortal soldier) was installed by then Prime Minister Indira Gandhi under the arch for the soldiers who gave up their lives in the Indo-Pakistan war of December 1971. This black marble memorial to the unknown soldier consists of a pedestal with a reversed rifle that has a military helmet on its butt. The words *Amar Jawan* in Hindi, are inscribed on all four sides of the memorial and the flags of the three defence services stand nearby.

There are four flames at the base of the memorial, one in each corner. However, only one flame, run on gas, burns throughout the year, while all four flames are lit on India's Republic Day on 26 January, and Independence Day on 15 August. The annual Republic Day parade held in Delhi on 26 January begins after the Prime Minister lays a wreath at the Amar Jawan Jyoti. Foreign dignitaries and heads of state visiting Delhi also pay tribute to the martyrs by laying wreaths at the Amar Jawan Jyoti.

Behind India Gate is a red sandstone canopy, now empty, built to house the statue of British King George V. The 15-metre high statue, looking westward in the direction of Rashtrapati Bhavan, then the Viceroy's House, stood in the canopy until

LOCATION:
At the eastern end of Rajpath, central Delhi. Nearest Metro Station: Central Secretariat.

1968 when it was transferred to Coronation Memorial Park in the far north region of Delhi. The statues of British viceroys such as Lord Willingdon and Lord Hardinge can also be found in this neglected walled garden originally designated as the location for the new imperial capital. Coronation Memorial Park was the site of the Delhi Durbar of 1911 during which the British monarch was proclaimed emperor of India.

India Gate is surrounded by lush green lawns which are popular with picnickers, particularly after sunset when the arch and the fountains in the area are floodlit. This is also the time when hawkers converge on the area, selling everything from balloons to snacks, ice cream and cold drinks. Close by is the Boat Club where visitors can hire boats and go boating in the canal running parallel to Rajpath.

India Gate is an imposing 42-metre high stone arch similar to the famous Arc-de-Triomphe in Paris.

INDIAN CHINESE CUISINE

Ask any Indian to describe Indian Chinese food and he is sure to mention *Chilli Chicken*, *American Chopsuey* and *Gobi Manchurian*. These three dishes are among the most popular of this fusion cuisine found all over India and even overseas, in areas where there is a high concentration of Indians. Other favourites are *Fried Rice*, *Garlic Chicken*, *Hot and Sour Soup* and deep-fried *Spring Rolls* with vegetable or chicken stuffing.

Indian Chinese cuisine is essentially Chinese food that has been Indianised with the addition of spices such as coriander powder, turmeric, cumin, red chilli powder, the spice blend garam masala, onion, green chillies, garlic and ginger. The end result is spicy, with gravy, making the food better suited to the Indian palate. Chicken, fish and mutton are the non-vegetarian options of choice in Indian Chinese cuisine.

There are plenty of vegetarian dishes, with cauliflower, called *gobi* in Hindi, being one of the most popular, particularly when it is combined with the thick brown Manchurian sauce. Another vegetarian variation of this dish is *Paneer Manchurian*, which is cottage cheese cooked in the Manchurian blend. This tasty sauce, a base for many Indian Chinese dishes, is prepared from stock, honey, corn starch, soy sauce and brown sugar. *Chilly Paneer* is a delectable fusion creation in which paneer is deep fried and sautéed with onion, capsicum and green chillies, after which it is simmered in a thick gravy comprising soy sauce, vinegar and black pepper.

Gobi Manchurian (left) and Chicken Noodles (opposite) are two popular dishes served in Indian Chinese restaurants.

Indian Chinese cuisine has its origins in the Chinese community of Calcutta (Kolkata). These Chinese immigrants, largely of Hakka descent, first arrived in the city in the late 1700s when it was the capital of British India. The Hakkas are Han Chinese from the Manchuria region of north-east China. Manchurian dishes in Indian Chinese cuisine derive their name from this region. The Calcutta Chinese worked on the docks and in the carpentry and leather business. It was much later that they got into the food business and by the 1960s, with the popularity of Chinese cuisine spreading to the general population, their restaurants and eateries had begun to thrive.

Today there are Indian Chinese restaurants all over India, and they can also be found in countries like the United States, Australia and Singapore. In Delhi, you can enjoy Indian Chinese cuisine at a number of restaurants such as Chopsticks, Fujiya, Zen, Drums of Heaven and Golden Dragon. Many of the 5-star hotels have their own Chinese restaurants such as House of Ming at the Taj Hotel and Tea House of the August Moon at Taj Palace Hotel where you can get authentic Chinese food as well as Indian Chinese favourites. There are also cheaper kiosk type outlets and mobile meal vans serving this hugely popular cuisine in the Indian capital. However, most Indians prefer to eat their Chinese food with forks and knives on normal size dinner plates, instead of eating out of small bowls with the aid of chopsticks.

JAMA MASJID

Perched on a hillock amidst the frenzy of old Delhi, or Shajahanabad, stands the majestic Jama Masjid, the largest mosque in India and a magnificent legacy of Mughal Emperor Shah Jahan's reign. The Jama Masjid, also known as Masjid-i-Jahan-Nama or 'Mosque with a view of the world', was the principal mosque in Shahjahanabad, the city Shah Jahan built as his capital in the 17th century to replace Agra. Built in sandstone and marble like other Mughal buildings, it dominates the old Delhi skyline with its three bulbous black and white marble domes flanked by lofty minarets. There are several other three-dome mosques such as Ghata Masjid and Sunehri Masjid in old Delhi, but the Jama Masjid remains the most distinctive, and is considered one of the finest examples of Mughal architecture because of the pleasing symmetry and harmony of its design.

Male devotees praying at the Jama Masjid.

Standing 10 metres above ground level in close proximity to the Red Fort, another vital landmark of Shah Jahan's kingdom, Jama Masjid is bounded by teeming bazaars on all sides. Broad flights of steps lead up to its three gateways which open into a capacious courtyard designed with squares of red sandstone, large enough to hold up to 25,000 devotees at a time. A marble tank used for washing hands and feet before prayers, is located at the centre of the courtyard.

The east gateway is the largest and the most impressive, an irregular octagon-shaped three-storeyed tower, also built in red sandstone. This was the entrance reserved for the Mughal emperors, while members of the public used the smaller gateways to the south and north. According to legend, Emperor Shah Jahan visited the mosque unannounced a day after it was completed and found a pile of rubble in the courtyard. Aghast mosque authorities, looking for ways to clear the mess quickly, requested devotees to

help out. With a large number pitching in, a task that would have ordinarily taken days was finished in a few hours. In present day, the east gate is used only on Fridays and on festivals such as *Id–ul–Fitr* and *Id–ul–Adha*. The main prayer hall, adorned with a series of arched alcoves and surmounted by the three domes, is situated at the west end of the courtyard facing Mecca.

The majestic domes and minarets of the Jama Masjid are a landmark in old Delhi.

The Jama Masjid, which was designed by the architect Ustad Khalil and constructed over six years from 1650 to 1656 at a cost of 1 million rupees, also houses relics of Prophet Muhammad. These relics, including the *Holy Qur'an* written on deerskin, a hair from the beard of the prophet, his sandal and his footprint in stone, are stored in the north-west corner of the mosque. The Jama Masjid is open to visitors in the morning and afternoon when prayers are not in session. The two minarets afford spectacular views of the city, but only the southern one is open to visitors, with women allowed to climb up only if accompanied by a male. An arcade running right along the courtyard also provides arresting views of the city. All visitors to the mosque have to be suitably attired with arms and legs covered as a mark of respect.

Devotees cleansing themselves before they enter the main prayer hall.

JANTAR MANTAR

Sandwiched between prosaic office buildings in the hub of Delhi's bureaucratic zone, stands a singular pink-coloured monument that goes by the name of Jantar Mantar. This is a fascinating observatory that was built in 1724 by King Maharajah Sawai Jai Singh ll of Jaipur. Dissatisfied with the existing astronomical tables and at the urging of Mughal Emperor Muhammad Shah (r. 1719-1748), this passionate astronomer set about creating new tables he called 'Zij Muhammad Shahe' after the emperor, and instruments that would be more accurate. Jantar Mantar in Delhi was the first of five observatories that Jai Singh established, the other four being in the north Indian cities of Jaipur (a city that he created), Ujjain, Varanasi and Mathura.

This 18th century observatory has enormous instruments created in masonry to tell the time and determine the position of celestial bodies.

The Delhi observatory has enormous instruments created in masonry, the material that Jai Singh preferred to brass. The largest of these devices is the *Samrat Yantra* or 'supreme instrument', a simple equal hour sundial that has curved quadrants on the sides of a triangular gnomon from which the time of day can be ascertained. Next to the *Samrat Yantra* is the *Misra Yantra*, meaning 'mixed instruments' for the different devices that it consists of. This instrument was used for meridian altitudes among other observations.

Lying behind the *Samrat Yantra* is the *Jai Prakash* which comprises of two concave hemispheres, one the reverse of the other, that was used to help determine the position of the sun and other celestial bodies. The *Ram Yantra* has two complementary circular structures, each with a central pole, that were used to determine the altitude of the sun. The other instruments include the *Dakshinottarabhitti-Yantra* and the *Agra Yantra*.

The Jantar Mantar observatory was damaged in the late 18th century when most of the marble used in the construction was vandalised. It was restored during extensive work carried out in 1852 and later in 1910. In present day, Jantar Mantar is not only a major tourist attraction in the city, but being close to the seat of government, it has become a favoured spot for public protests and hunger strikes.

LOCATION:
Sansad Marg
(Parliament Street)
Nearest Metro
Station: Patel
Chowk.

JAWAHARLAL NEHRU STADIUM AND THE 2010 COMMONWEALTH GAMES

In history-suffused Delhi which has seen a succession of rulers and dynasties, ancient tombs and monuments can be found in the most unlikely places. One such place is next to the running track at the Jawaharlal Nehru Stadium, Delhi's biggest sporting facility and one of the largest in the country. This stadium, which has a seating capacity of 100,000 spectators, is exceeded in size only by the Salt Lake Stadium in Kolkata (formerly Calcutta) which can seat up to 120,000.

The multi-purpose Jawaharlal Nehru Stadium, named after India's first prime minister, was built for the 1982 Asian Games that Delhi hosted. Since then, this premier sporting arena has held countless national and international events such as the 1991 Junior Asian Athletics and the 2004 World Half-Marathon. Its crowning glory will be the 2010 Commonwealth Games which Delhi will host, an honour for India, the second Asian country to do so after Malaysia. The Jawaharlal Nehru Stadium will be the venue of the opening and closing ceremonies for the mega event, the most prestigious to be hosted by India.

Delhi has plans to remodel the entire Jawaharlal Nehru Stadium to bring it on par with international standards, as part of preparatory plans for the Games. Other state-owned sports facilities in Delhi, such as the Indira Gandhi Indoor Stadium, the Siri Fort Sports Complex and the Yamuna Sports Complex will also be expanded and spruced up for the event while new facilities, including a games village and the Thyagaraj Sports Complex, will be constructed.

At the Jawaharlal Nehru Stadium, the synthetic track will be refurbished, though a 16-sided tomb circa 16th century that stands close to it will remain untouched. This tomb, along with two others hailing from the 14th to 16th centuries located in the vicinity of the stadium, were preserved during the construction of the stadium in the 1980s. A 14th-century tomb stands between gates 9 and 10, while an early Mughal period tomb, surmounted by a *chhatri* or decorative canopy, is located to the north.

The Jawaharlal Nehru Stadium is significant for other reasons too. It is the headquarters of the Indian Olympics Association and a state-owned cricket academy, the first of its kind, set up

LOCATION:
Lodhi Road,
south Delhi.
Tel: 24369400-01

by the Sports Authority of India. The stadium is also a popular venue for glamorous Bollywood concerts featuring India's top film stars such as Shah Rukh Khan, who have performed elaborate song and dance routines to a sell-out crowd here.

KALKAJI **TEMPLE**

The origin of the Kalkaji Temple, dedicated to Hindu Goddess Kalka Devi or Kali, in south Delhi is steeped in legend. One tale talks about a local farmer who discovered to his chagrin that his cow had stopped producing milk. When he followed the cow to pasture to learn the cause of this development, he realised that she was giving all her milk to Goddess Kali. This prompted him to build a temple in the area and dedicate it to the goddess. Because of the goddess' love for milk, he began bathing the idol in milk every day, a ritual which continues to this day.

According to another story passed down through the generations, a weary king who had suffered defeat at the hands of an invading army stopped a while to rest at the site of the Kalkaji Temple. He dozed off, and while sleeping, dreamt about Goddess Kali telling him to venture again into battle against his enemy. When he woke up, he gathered his troops and followed the instructions from his dream, emerging victorious this time. To express his gratitude, he erected the temple at the site in honour of the goddess who is a reincarnation of Goddess Durga, the Mother Goddess.

It is believed that an ancient temple lies buried beneath the present structure, the oldest part of which dates back to 1764.

Devotees visit the Kalkaji Temple to seek the blessings of Hindu Goddess Kalka Devi, a reincarnation of the Mother Goddess.

Additions were made to it in 1816 when Mirza Raja Kedarnath, who belonged to then Mughal Emperor Akbar Shah II's court, had a dome and 12 outer rooms constructed. Rest houses for pilgrims were built in the temple complex in the 20th century. The temple has also witnessed several historic events, being strategically located on the outskirts of the city. In 1805, Maratha troops under Jaswant Rao Holkar, massed near Kalkaji Temple before heading into the city. There was also activity around the Kalkaji Temple during the Sepoy Mutiny of 1857, and again during the partition of the Indian subcontinent in 1947.

The Kalkaji Temple is a simple building of white marble and granite, devoid of lavish ornamentation. The black stone idol of the goddess stands at the centre of the inner sanctum covered with red brocade cloth and enclosed by a marble railing. Devotees come in droves to pay their respects to the goddess during the nine-day Navratri celebrations held in October, just before Diwali, the festival of lights, when a large fair is held at the temple. A smaller fair is held in the vicinity every Tuesday when the temple receives a large number of devotees. Villagers also throng to the temple after their annual wheat harvest to make an offering of the crop to the goddess. The most important ritual at the temple is the bathing of the idol in milk every day. This is followed by the recitation of hymns.

LOCATION:
Kalkaji, south Delhi, near Nehru Place and the Baha'i Temple.

LAKSHMI NARAYAN **(BIRLA)** MANDIR

The beehive-shaped towers are one of the most striking features of Lakshmi Narayan Mandir, built in 1938.

One of the most popular Hindu temples in Delhi, the Lakshmi Narayan Mandir is dedicated to Hindu God Vishnu (also known as Narayan), the preserver, and Lakshmi, the goddess of wealth, hence its name Lakshmi Narayan. This imposing sandstone structure which dominates Mandir Marg, the road in central Delhi that it is located on, was built in 1938 in the Nagara style of architecture. It is replete with beehive-shaped towers representative of the Nagara style, carvings, friezes and sculptures depicting scenes from Hindu mythology. The temple's walls are covered with writings from Hindu scriptures like the *Bhagavad Gita* and the *Upanishads*.

The sanctum sanctorum of the temple, situated under its central 50-metre high tower, holds idols of Vishnu and Lakshmi. Surrounding this chamber are smaller shrines dedicated to other gods of the Hindu pantheon such as Shiva, Ganesha, Krishna, Durga and Hanuman. The ancient Hindu scriptures, the *Vedas*, are also enshrined in this temple, while there is a small chamber dedicated to the Buddha, complete with fresco paintings depicting scenes from his life. Miniature rock temples and an artificial landscape with mountains and fountains at the rear of the temple provide a pleasant play area for visiting children.

The Lakshmi Narayan Mandir was built by the Birla family of industrialists and is one of several temples established by them across the country. It is popularly known as Birla Mandir after the family. It was inaugurated by Mahatma Gandhi, better known as the father of the nation for his role in India's freedom struggle, who insisted that the temple be open to people of all sections of society, including the poor and underprivileged.

The Lakshmi Narayan Mandir draws devotees throughout the year but is particularly busy during the festival of Janmashtami, when the birth anniversary of Lord Krishna is celebrated on a grand scale, and Diwali, the sparkling Hindu festival of lights.

LOCATION:
Mandir Marg, west of Connaught Place.
Nearest Metro Station: Jhandewalan.

LAL QILA (RED FORT)

Luxuriant brocade, velvet and silk draperies, Kashmiri carpets, silver columns to support marble canopied thrones and golden pillars ornamented with gems; such was the splendour of the Lal Qila or Red Fort, the fortified palace of Mughal Emperor Shah Jahan in Delhi, built after the city became the capital of his empire in 1648.

Today, less than one-fourth of the Lal Qila, the crowning glory of Shah Jahan's Shahjahanabad, (see Seven Cities of Delhi, page 144) is open to the public. The rest is occupied by the Indian army which moved into the fort after the Sepoy Mutiny of 1857. Much of the Lal Qila was plundered by invaders in the 18th century, and many buildings were demolished by the Indian Army in 1858 to make way for barracks. What is left of the once resplendent fort, a UNESCO World Heritage site, is in a state of disrepair. But despite the ravages wrought by traumatic historical interludes, the Lal Qila still retains a vestige of its former grandeur, visible in the architectural lines of its imposing arched Lahore Gate, Mumtaz Mahal, Khas Mahal, Diwan-i-Am and the Diwan-i-Khas, the grandest building of them all. The history of the Lal Qila is featured in a sound and light show held daily in the fort complex.

Lal Qila is an octagon-shaped citadel on the banks of the Yamuna River. It stretches 2.4 km across one end of Shahjahanabad or old Delhi, and comprises a series of pavilions which hold Shah Jahan's palace buildings. The fort's walls, built of red sandstone, are punctuated by two towering gateways, Lahore Gate facing Chandni Chowk and Delhi Gate, facing old sections of the city. It is from the three-storey Lahore Gate, the more imposing of the two gates, that the Prime Minister of India addresses the country every year on Independence Day on 15 August.

Lahore Gate leads on to the Chhatta Chowk covered bazaar and after a few yards, the Naubat or Naqqar Khana (Drum Room), which is where, in the past, all visitors to the fort were welcomed. Visitors in Shah Jahan's time had to dismount from their elephants at the Naqqar Khana and then walk to the Diwan-i-Am or the Hall of Public Audience nearby. Musicians sitting in the gallery above the reception area would play lively melodies on kettledrums and trumpets at the arrival or departure

The Red Fort took almost 10 years to complete and cost 6 million rupees. It was designed by Shah Jahan's master architects Ustad Hamid and Ustad Ahmed, and was completed in 1657.

LOCATION:
Eastern end of Chandni Chowk, old Delhi.
Tel: 23274580.
Closed on Monday.
Nearest Metro Station: Chandni Chowk

of the emperor and important visitors. This gallery now houses the Indian War Memorial Museum.

Shah Jahan would meet with members of the public at the elegant Diwan-i-Am, a pavilion with three open sides, designed with sandstone colonnades and cusped arches, and embellished with intricate gold stucco work. The Mughal emperor, who went by the title Zille-I-Ilahi or Shadow of God on Earth, used to spend two hours every morning in this hall for his public meetings, sitting on his marble canopied throne known as the Nishan-i-Zille-I-Ilahi and holding forth on administration issues, or addressing grievances. A richly ornamented inlaid *pietra dura* (hard stone) panel depicting the Greek god Orpheus with wild animals, believed to have originated in Italy, lies behind the throne.

The private domain of the emperor included the Mumtaz Mahal, used by Shah Jahan's favourite daughter Jahanara Begum. It now houses the Museum of Archaeology; Rang Mahal, which was the palace for the royal women; Khas Mahal, the emperor's palace with special rooms for prayer, sleeping and living; the royal bathing area known as *hammams*; the pearl mosque Moti Masjid, made of marble and built by Mughal Emperor Aurangzeb in 1659 for his personal use; Shahi Burj, the private working area of Shah Jahan; and the Diwan-i-Khas, the ornate Hall of Private Audience standing on a high pavilion.

This gilded hall, reserved for the emperor's audience with nobles, housed the priceless, golden, jewel-encrusted Peacock Throne, which derived its name from the canopy held by 12 pillars decorated with peacocks. This stunning piece of workmanship, fashioned from 1,150 kg of gold and 230 kg of precious stones, was plundered by Persian invader Nadir Shah in 1739. Fragments of the Peacock Throne were later salvaged and incorporated in the Persian Nadiri Peacock Throne kept in the Gulestan Palace in Teheran. The Diwan-i-Khas also had a striking silver ceiling which was looted by Maratha invaders in 1760. A celebrated verse by 13th century Sufi poet Amir Khusro, inscribed under the cornice in a corner, aptly describes the magnificence of the Diwan-i-Khas in Shah Jahan's Lal Qila:

'Agar firdous bar rue zamin ast
Hamin ast o hamin ast o hamin ast.'

(If there is paradise on Earth, it is this, it is this, it is this.)

Looking through the beautiful lattice work into a courtyard of the Red Fort.

LODHI GARDEN

Lodhi Garden is a green oasis that allows visitors to walk through history, past relics from the days of the Delhi Sultanate as well as the Mughal period. Besides its ponds, fountains, shady trees and walkways, Lodhi Garden is home to a mosque and the tombs of rulers of the Sayyid and Lodhi dynasties that ruled the Delhi Sultanate in the 15th and 16th centuries. It also holds the National Bonsai Park with its exotic collection of miniature trees and plants.

Tall and stately palm trees flank the walkways of Lodhi Garden.

At the centre of the garden is the imposing domed *Bara Gumbad* (Big Dome), which has an adjoining mosque made of ashlar stone, and is designed with tapering minarets. The mosque was built in 1494 during the reign of Sikander Lodhi. To the north is *Sheesh Gumbad* (Glass Gumbad), which resembles *Bara Gumbad* in its square structure and double-storeyed façade. It was originally covered in blue coloured tiles, traces of which are visible even today.

Located in the south-western section of the extensive garden is the tomb of Mohammed Shah, third ruler of the Sayyid dynasty, who died in 1444. The tomb, an excellent example of the prevailing architectural style later used in the construction of the Taj Mahal and other Mughal monuments, consists of an octagonal shaped chamber that holds the graves of Mohammed Shah and other family members. This inner chamber is surrounded by arched verandahs. The garden also holds the tomb of Sikander Lodhi (r. 1489-1517), which is enclosed in a walled garden. Beyond it is an eight-tiered stone bridge, known as Athpula, which was built during the Tughlaq period.

This historic garden was renamed Lady Willingdon Park in 1936, but reverted back to its original name in 1947 when India gained independence from the British. Adjoining Lodhi Garden is the India International Centre (IIC), set up in December 1958 as an autonomous convention centre which, according to its charter, 'promotes understanding and amity between different world communities'. In keeping with its charter, IIC organises international and national conferences as well as cultural programmes, book readings, film screenings and art exhibitions for its members and the general public.

LOCATION:
Lodhi Road,
south Delhi

LUTYENS' **NEW DELHI**

Delhi, the site of seven medieval cities, got its eighth city, New Delhi, in the early 20th century. New Delhi, built by the British colonialists as their capital in India, was a city of wide tree-lined avenues, fountains, gracious pink and cream government buildings and single-storey bungalows that combined Indian motifs and Western Classicism in a harmonious synthesis. It was a regal enclave befitting the imperial rulers, created by architects Edwin Landseer Lutyens and Herbert Baker.

It was during the historic Durbar of 12 December 1911 that British monarch King George V made the unexpected announcement to transfer the capital from Calcutta to Delhi. Delhi was selected for its central location, particularly its proximity to Simla, the summer capital of the British rulers, and its historic track record as the seat of the Muslim dynasties that ruled medieval India. An ambitious plan to build a magnificent new city reflecting the supremacy of the British Empire, from where India could be ruled for centuries to come, was developed.

Lutyens, best known for his designs of English country houses, was appointed to the Delhi Town Planning Committee and became its chief architect in 1912. After surveying the lay of the land on elephant back, he selected the site around Raisina Hill, a wilderness dotted with villages, as the focal point for the new city and built it 'as an Englishman dressed for the climate'.

The area, owned by the Maharajah of Jaipur, was chosen for its openness and its healthier aspect, being far from swamps unlike north Delhi, the original choice for the capital. The designated land was bought by the government, cleared and developed with buildings of historical interest such as the 18th century Sunehri Bagh Mosque, left untouched. Lutyens and Baker designed a geometric grid of roads and landscaped roundabouts, with its hub the 3.2-km-long boulevard called Kingsway (now Rajpath) that had the imposing Viceregal Lodge atop Raisina Hill at its west end and the prominent India Gate at its east end. At the base of Raisina Hill was Vijay Chowk (Victory Square, originally called the Central Vista), flanked by the two Secretariat Buildings, while to the north lay the circular colonnaded Council Chamber, now Sansad Bhavan or Parliament House.

The hub of British New Delhi was Kingsway (now Rajpath) with the imposing Viceregal Lodge atop Raisina Hill flanked by the two Secretariat Buildings.

Each avenue was named after Indian leaders such as freedom fighter Motilal Nehru, British governor general Lord Dalhousie, and Mughal emperors Akbar and Aurangzeb. The roads were shaded by indigenous trees like the Java Plum (Syzygium cumini), Neem (Azadirachta indica) and Tamarind (Tamarindus indica), to keep out the blazing Indian sun. To the south of Viceregal Lodge were built the colonial bungalows with their deep verandahs, set in lush gardens. Indian princes were accommodated in royal residences such as Hyderabad House and Baroda House, both designed by Lutyens. A few kilometres away, the upscale shopping centre of Connaught Place was established.

The open, healthy environment of central Delhi made it the ideal choice for the imperial capital.

It took Lutyens and his associate Herbert Baker almost 20 years to complete the New Delhi project, delayed because of World War 1 and other factors. Several local contractors were involved in the endeavour, notably Sujan Singh and his son Sobha, the grandfather and father of celebrated modern-day writer Khushwant Singh. As many as 30,000 labourers were employed in the construction, and a railway line was especially created to ferry millions of tons of stone and other raw material to the site. The building project stirred up controversy in the country with Indian nationalists condemning the wasteful expenditure. But despite the odds, New Delhi was formally inaugurated in 1931. Ironically, the British government, which had anticipated a long innings in its new seat of power, lasted only 16 years. By August 1947, New Delhi was the capital of a free India.

MAHATMA GANDHI'S
RAJ GHAT AND OTHER MEMORIALS

It was on 31 January 1948 that Mohandas Karamchand Gandhi, revered as Mahatma (great soul) in the country, was cremated on the banks of the Yamuna River, a day after his horrific assassination by a Hindu fanatic. Gandhi's killing shattered newly independent India, still struggling with the traumatic

LOCATION:

Mahatma Gandhi Marg (Ring Road). Raj Ghat , Tel: 23311793 Closed on Monday. Nearest Metro Station: Pragati Maidan

consequences of the partition of the subcontinent that took place just months earlier. The site of the cremation, converted into a memorial named Raj Ghat, has become a national shrine where members of the public, as well as visiting foreign heads of state, go to pay their respects to the great leader given the title 'Father of the Nation', for the pivotal role he played in India's freedom struggle. In Hinduism, it is considered auspicious to hold cremations on the banks of holy rivers such as the Yamuna—it is believed that the soul attains salvation through this ritual.

At the centre of a serene landscaped garden on the west bank of the Yamuna River stands the simple black marble platform strewn with flowers and encircled by grey stones, which marks the site of Gandhi's cremation. Some of the trees in the garden have exalted origins, having been bestowed by illustrious visitors to Raj Ghat, including US President Dwight Eisenhower who planted an American flannel bush sapling in December 1959.

The black marble memorial is engraved with Mahatma Gandhi's last words, "Hey Ram".

An eternal flame burns at the memorial, on which are engraved the last words uttered by Gandhi, 'Hey Ram' (Hindi for 'Oh God!'), before he collapsed on the grounds of the colonial bungalow Birla House, while on his way to his daily prayer meeting. Birla House, on Tees January Marg, has been converted into the Gandhi Smriti Museum which has a Martyr's Column erected at the spot where he was assassinated. The room that Gandhi resided in during his last days, has been preserved in its original condition, while his last steps to the prayer meeting in the back garden have been delineated. The avenue, Tees January, is named after Gandhi's death anniversary.

The memorial at Raj Ghat is contained within an open-top walled enclosure, which is reached by way of a broad walkway leading in from the main gate. The sandstone walls of the enclosure are inscribed with samples of Gandhi's writings in different languages. A prayer meeting is held at Raj Ghat at 5 pm every Friday, the day Gandhi was killed, and special prayers are scheduled on 2 October, Gandhi's birth anniversary and 30 January, his death anniversary.

Across the road from Raj Ghat is Gandhi Darshan, a small museum that holds paintings and photographs from Gandhi's life, while a short distance away is the Gandhi National Museum which displays precious Gandhi memorabilia, including a South African sculpture of the leader, the bamboo staff he carried on his Salt March in March to April 1930, the *dhoti* (a long wraparound garment worn at the midriff) he was wearing the day he died, as well as letters and diaries.

Standing close to Raj Ghat are a number of memorials set in blooming gardens on the banks of the Yamuna River, erected in memory of other leaders of independent India. These include Shanti Vana, a memorial to Jawaharlal Nehru, the first prime minister, who ruled from 1947 until his death of a heart attack on 27 May 1964; Vijay Ghat for Lal Bahadur Shastri (Prime Minister: 1964-1966); Shakti Sthal, for Indira Gandhi, Nehru's daughter (Prime Minister: 1966-1977, 1980-1984); Kisan Ghat for Chaudhary Charan Singh (Prime Minister: 1979); Vir Bhumi, for Rajiv Gandhi, Indira Gandhi's son (Prime Minister: 1984-1989). The 47-year-old Rajiv Gandhi was assassinated by a suicide bomber while he was campaigning for elections in the southern state of Tamil Nadu in May 1991.

MARKETS AND MALLS

When it comes to shopping, Delhi has plenty to offer, from the warren of narrow lanes laden with goodies in the historic markets of Chandni Chowk to the British-created upscale shopping centre Connaught Place. Where once these two areas dominated Delhi's retail business, today there is a market in every neighbourhood of the city offering an array of indigenous and foreign made products. Shopping malls have also mushroomed in Delhi and its satellite towns Gurgaon and Noida, offering international branded goods in a modern Western style shopping environment.

LOCATION:

Markets —all over Delhi, notably, Karol Bagh in the west zone, and Lajpat Nagar Central Market and Sarojini Nagar, in the south. The mentioned markets are closed on Mondays.

Malls—Ansal Plaza, Khel Gaon Marg, south Delhi.

In Delhi markets, high-priced stores are juxtaposed with streetside stalls and pavement kiosks selling bric-à-brac, providing an interesting melange for residents to choose from. In the late evening, after closing hours and on the weekly off day for the established stores, these markets are transformed into flea markets patronised by residents looking for a good bargain.

Karol Bagh's famous Ajmal Khan Market is one of the oldest in the city, established by Punjabis who fled Pakistan during the traumatic days of the Partition of the subcontinent in 1947.

From a single road lined with stores, this market has witnessed exponential growth, becoming a nucleus for wedding attire and accessories, gold and diamond jewellery, silk, cotton and other textiles, *saris* and readymade Indian garments. Renowned stores in this market include Jainsons Westend, Westside, Ram Chandra Kishan Chandra and Zohra Emporium. Karol Bagh is also reputed for its labyrinthine Ghaffar Market, which draws crowds for its profusion of imported goods, from watches, to cosmetics to blankets and electronic goods. For spices and dry fruits stores, Roopak's is a particular favourite with housewives because of the superior quality of its house brand products.

In the late evenings and on off days, Delhi's markets are transformed into flea markets, with hawkers selling their wares on the pavement.

Ajmal Khan Road's counterpart in south Delhi is the Central Market at Lajpat Nagar, best known for its ethnic wear, especially *salwar kameez* suits popular with Delhi residents. These can be bought ready made or they can be tailored in this market which offers a number of textile stores and tailoring units. For Western attire preferred by youngsters, there is no better place than the Sarojini Nagar Market which has a large selection of trendy garments and accessories manufactured for export to Western countries which find their way into this market as leftovers from surplus production. Prices are low and negotiable though quality is not first rate. Sarojini Nagar market, originally established for the residents of the adjacent Sarojini Nagar government colony, also has a number of reputed retail establishments such as Liberty and Bata Shoes, Paradise Sarees and Lee.

South Extension and M Block Market in Greater Kailash offer more trendy and stylish clothes, shoes and accessories, while Ambawatta Complex in Mehrauli and Santushti Complex in Chanakyapuri offer exclusive designer wear as well as pottery, furnishings and linen. Shyam Ahuja and Anokhi in the Santushti complex have an elegant range of home furnishings, and Good Earth keeps striking designs in crockery and silverware.

Yashwant Place in Chanakyapuri specialises in leather goods which are also available at Hidesign and D Minsen & Co in Connaught Place. Khan Market is popular with book lovers and also has a plethora of lamp and lighting shops, while the Basant Lok Market in Vasant Vihar and the Saket markets in south Delhi draw crowds because of their cinema halls, with the multiplex PVR Anupam being specially favoured for its wide selection of new English and Hindi releases.

Ansal Plaza, Delhi's first shopping mall located near South Extension, is favoured for its American style department store Shopper's Store and other upmarket outlets such as Music World which keeps a wide selection of music CDs and DVDs. Metro Walk is Delhi's largest mall spread over 18,580 square metres in the Rohini area of west Delhi. It is part of an ambitious retail and leisure complex that includes the Adventure Island amusement park. Metro Walk, which overlooks an artificial lake, houses retail stores such as Reebok, Nike and Pantaloon, and offers a range of cuisines including Indian, Chinese and fast food outlets such as McDonald's and KFC. More malls can be found in south and east Delhi and in the satellite towns of Gurgaon and Noida (see Gurgaon and Noida, page 58).

MIRZA **GHALIB**

Delhi was home to one of the greatest Urdu poets of the 19th century, Mirza Asadullah Baig Khan, better known by his pen name Ghalib. A member of the court of the last Mughal Emperor Bahadur Shah II, the self-taught Ghalib was a brilliant writer who was able to reach out to the elite classes as well as the masses.

His poignant writing delved into romance, his own fluctuating fortunes, the death of his seven children, as well as the metamorphosis of society under the British. His exceptional works, many of which have been translated into different

The entrance to Mirza Ghalib ki Haveli. Today, it houses a small museum displaying the poet's memorabilia.

LOCATION:

Mirza Ghalib Haveli is in Chandni Chowk, old Delhi. Nearest Metro Station: Chandni Chowk. Mirza Ghalib's Tomb and Academy are in Nizamuddin West, off Mathura Road. Nearest Metro Station: Pragati Maidan

languages, include a 10-volume collection of poems called *Diwan-i-Ghalib*, his letters to relatives, friends and his favourite pupil Dad Khan Sayyah, compiled in *Urdu-e-Muallah*, and works of prose such as *Naam-I-Ghalib*, *Latief-I-Ghalib* and *Daupshe Kawaiyam*. Many of Ghalib's love poems are stirring ghazals (light classical songs) popularised by Indian singers Jagjit Singh and Talat Aziz, while his remarkable life has been chronicled in films, plays and a television serial.

This pre-eminent writer in the Urdu language, who also made an impact with his work in Persian, was born in Agra and moved to Delhi soon after his marriage to Umrao Begum at the age of 13. The young Ghalib initially stayed with his father-in-law and later lived in rented accommodation in Chandni Chowk, the bustling centre of Mughal Emperor Shah Jahan's Shajahanabad city. It was only at the end of his life, in 1860, that he bought his own *haveli* or private courtyard house in Chandni Chowk. Mirza Ghalib ki Haveli, situated in Gali Qasim Jaan, Ballimaran, was Ghalib's home until his death in 1869. A typical private house of the Mughal period, it was designed with a decorative façade that included a central arch at the entrance, arched corridors, an open courtyard flanked by rooms and sandstone flooring.

Like many of the other *havelis* in Chandni Chowk, Mirza Ghalib ki Haveli was used as a commercial establishment until the government restored it to its former beauty and converted it into a memorial for the poet on his birth anniversary on 27 December 2000. The *haveli* has a small museum which displays Ghalib memorabilia, including his emotive letters, his books, couplets and some personal belongings. A full-size replica of the poet smoking a hookah, a type of water pipe, brings him to life in his final place of residence.

A few kilometres away, in the colony of Nizamuddin near Nizamuddin's Shrine, stands the Ghalib Academy, established in 1969 on the poet's death centenary, by physician and philanthropist Hakeem Abdul Hameed. The academy houses a library and a museum which has a valuable collection of photographs of the poet's life as well as those of literary luminaries of the 19th century. Mirza Ghalib's tomb, a simple white marble edifice, is adjacent to the academy and the prominent 64-pillar Chausath Khamba monument (see Nizamuddin's Shrine, page 114).

MITHAI (**SWEETMEAT**) SHOPS

Like other Indians, Delhiites love local sweets such as *rasmalai*, *gulab jamun*, *laddoos*, *kaju burfi*, *kalakand*, *jalebis*, *gajar* (carrot) *halwa* and *kulfi* which they consume after dinner as a dessert or even as a snack during the day. Demand for sweets goes up tenfold during festivals particularly Diwali, the Hindu festival of lights, when most people celebrate by distributing them to friends and family.

Indian sweets are available at specialty *mithai* shops, most of which provide basic cafeteria-style seating where customers can sit and enjoy the sweets if they wish, along with their favourite savouries such as *samosas*, *aloo tikkis* and *chaat*. The oldest of these shops is Ghantewala (bell ringer) in Chandni Chowk, old Delhi, which has been run by the same family since 1790 and is now in its 11th generation. According to popular lore, the shop, which catered to Mughal emperors, was named after a royal elephant which liked the sweets so much it would come to the shop regularly and stand outside ringing the bell around its neck until it was fed. Ghantewala produces all its sweets in pure ghee (clarified butter) to ensure the high quality of its products. It is famous for its *sohan halwa* made from sprouts.

Indian sweets are flavoured with saffron and are decorated with silver foil.

LOCATION:

All over Delhi, notably Bengali Market, Chandni Chowk and Karol Bagh.

Other popular *mithai* shops are Haldiram Bhujiawala, Annapoorna, Nathu's, Bikaner's and Bengali Sweets, all of which have several branches in the city. Annapoorna is a Bengali sweet shop which is part of a chain from the state of West Bengal. It is particularly famous for its *mishti doi*, a type of sweet yoghurt that is made with milk and sugar and is fermented overnight in an earthenware jar. It is a favourite dessert in the states of West Bengal and Orissa.

Roshan di Kulfi in Karol Bagh is renowned for its ice-cream-style sweet called *kulfi*, which is made from milk that has been thickened and mixed with crushed nuts. *Kulfi* is served with *falooda*—a kind of vermicelli made of corn flour—and topped with rose flavoured syrup and crushed ice. Hot *jalebis*, spiral shaped, orange-coloured sweets that are deep fried and soaked in sugar syrup, are especially enjoyed in winter when accompanied by a cup of tea or coffee. Old & Famous Jalebiwala in Chandni Chowk is a popular outlet for this sweet that it is named after.

Indian sweets typically come flavoured with saffron and are decorated with an ultra thin covering of silver foil called *vark*. This is edible and is perfectly safe for consumption. The silver foil, so fine that it crumbles when touched, is considered an enhancement for the sweets though it has no taste or smell.

Ghantewala is one of the oldest *mithai* shops in Delhi.

MUGHLAI CUISINE

A favourite with Delhi residents as well as tourists, Mughlai cuisine is essentially an amalgam of two different foods, Punjabi and Mughal. During the period of their rule in Delhi, from the 16th to 19th centuries, the Mughals popularised meat dishes prepared in yoghurt, clarified butter, dry fruits and spices. Later, after the partition of the Indian subcontinent in 1947, when people from Punjab state settled down in Delhi, they brought with them their own way of cooking and their distinctive flavours and spices. The two combined to create exotic Mughlai cuisine, with dishes such as *tandoori* chicken, butter chicken, chicken *tikka*, *seekh kebab*, *dal makhani*, *tandoori roti*, *naan* and *biryani* becoming all-time favourites.

The word *tandoori* is derived from *tandoor*, a large circular clay oven fuelled by charcoal. The heat from the burning charcoal rises right through the oven, heating its walls and the open centre in which the chicken and other meat dishes are grilled on skewers. Breads like *tandoori roti* and *naan* are placed on the hot interior walls where they are slow-cooked to perfection. Mughlai food tastes best accompanied by coriander chutney, spicy onion salad dressed with lemon, pickle and spiced yoghurt called *raita*. A variation of Mughlai cuisine is known as Frontier cuisine, which refers to the food originating in the North West Frontier Province of Pakistan. Frontier cuisine, which has a strong Persian influence, is primarily served at specialty restaurants in five-star hotels along with Mughlai varieties.

Tandoori Chicken or Murg Tandoori

Tandoori chicken is a succulent dish in which the chicken is marinated in yoghurt, garlic, ginger, lime juice and a medley of spices including turmeric, red chilli powder, coriander powder, cumin powder and *garam masala*. Some cooks prefer to use permitted artificial colours to give the chicken its delightful red hue. After it has been marinated, the chicken is placed in the *tandoor* and cooked until it is red and brown on the outside, soft and juicy on the inside. *Tandoori machchi* or fish is prepared in a similar fashion and is just as delectable.

Mughlai cuisine is an amalgam of the rich flavours of Punjabi and Mughal food.

Butter Chicken or Murg Makhani

Known as *murg makhani* locally, this consists of pre-roasted chunks of boneless chicken soaked in a rich creamy gravy—the essence of the dish and what gives it its name. All the ingredients used in *tandoori* chicken, along with onions, tomato puree, cream and whole spices such as peppercorn, cinnamon, bay leaves, cloves and cardamom go into this time-consuming preparation. Almonds, raisins and other dry fruits can be added to enrich the gravy. *Paneer makhani* is a vegetarian variation.

Chicken Tikka

Tiny chunks of marinated boneless chicken that are skewered and grilled in the *tandoor* are called chicken *tikka*. Chicken *tikka masala*, hugely popular in the United Kingdom, is a spicy concoction which like butter chicken involves simmering pre-cooked chicken *tikkas* in spicy gravy.

Seekh Kebab

Seekh kebabs are made from mince meat which is placed on skewers and then cooked in the *tandoor*. The meat, chicken or mutton, is flavoured with spices, onion, garlic, ginger, green chillies and coriander leaves and then pressed onto the skewers. *Seekh kebabs* make a delicious snack or a main course, when they can be eaten accompanied by *tandoori* chicken, *naan*, salad, chutney and *raita*. There are a number of variations in kebabs including *reshmi kebab* and *shammi kebab*.

Marinated chicken is cooked in the *tandoor* till it is red and brown on the outside, tender on the inside.

Dal Makhani

A meal of *tandoori* chicken and *seekh kebab* would not be complete without *dal makhani*, a vegetarian lentil-based dish made from black gram, Bengal gram and kidney beans. *Dal makhani* is slow cooked to perfection, and requires a minimum of spices but a large quantity of tomato puree, butter and cream, which give it its rich flavour. Cooking styles vary for this dish, with some people leaving out the kidney beans while others prefer to use an abundance of onions, garlic, ginger and green chillies for added punch.

Chicken/Mutton Biryani

This is a casserole-style concoction of meat, rice, spices and dry fruits that has a captivating taste and aroma. Chunks of meat are pre-cooked with onions, tomatoes, garlic and ginger and then mixed with half cooked rice. This combination is simmered on a slow fire and infused with a generous helping of dry fruits and spices such as cinnamon and cardamom. Saffron combined with milk gives the biryani its distinctive reddish tinge. *Biryani*, accompanied by *raita* and onion salad, is a meal in itself.

Tandoori Roti and Naan

A type of flat bread that is an essential accompaniment in a Mughlai meal, the *tandoori roti* is made from wheat flour combined with plain flour, water and salt. It is cooked in the *tandoor* until crisp. *Naan*, on the other hand, is prepared from white flour leavened with yeast. It is softer than the *tandoori roti* and can be prepared plain, with a dollop of butter for butter *naan*, or stuffed with potatoes and other fillings for the stuffed version. A delightful variation is garlic *naan*.

There are numerous restaurants, small eateries and streetside stalls serving Mughlai cuisine in Delhi. Among the most popular are Karim's, which has a dine-in outlet in old Delhi and one at Hazrat Nizamuddin in south Delhi; Moti Mahal in old Delhi, Pindi and Gulati on Pandara Road, and for a more classy experience, the Great Kebab Factory at Hotel Radisson, the Dhaba at Claridges and the internationally renowned, award-winning restaurant Bukhara at the Maurya Sheraton Hotel (see Bukhara Restaurant, page 27).

Karim's in old Delhi has been run by one family for almost 100 years and is synonymous with the best of Mughlai cuisine. It was in 1913 that Haji Karimuddin set up the Karim Hotel near Jama Masjid with the intention of serving 'royal food to the common man'. Today, its name is associated with spicy chicken and mutton *tandoori* fare prepared, as its present owner-chef Aleemuddin Ahmed proudly claims, from age-old recipes and with an assortment of spices, sometimes as many as 33 in a single dish.

NATIONAL **MUSEUM**

A stately building on the corner of Janpath and Maulana Azad Road in central Delhi, the National Museum of India is the premier museum in the country with over 200,000 exhibits covering 5,000 years of history and culture. The museum has an impressive collection of pre-historic archaeological artefacts, jewellery, miniature paintings, ancient manuscripts, coins, tribal art, textiles, Central Asian antiquities, arms and armour. Deserving special mention is the gallery on the Harappan or Indus Valley Civilisation which has thousands of items of pottery, seals, tablets, weights and measures, jewellery, terracotta figurines, toys and copper tools belonging to South Asia's first known urban settlement that existed from 2800 to 1900 BC. The National Museum was formally inaugurated on 15 August 1949, but it functioned in the Presidential Palace Rashtrapati Bhavan until 18 December 1960 when it moved to its own premises.

> **LOCATION:**
> Janpath. Tel: 23019272. Website: http://www. nationalmuseumindia. gov.in/.
> Closed on Monday. Nearest Metro Station: Central Secretariat

The National Museum is spread across three levels with six galleries located on the ground floor, five on the first floor and two on the second floor. It is best to begin any exploration of the museum on the ground floor with its extraordinary prehistoric section. The piece de resistance of the extensive Indus Valley display is the renowned circa 2,500 BC dancing girl from Mohenjo-Daro, skilfully crafted from bronze. The Indus Valley Civilisation is also represented in the ground floor gallery devoted to jewellery, where all kinds of objects of adornment worn through the various stages of Indian history are displayed. This treasure trove has over 200 items dating from the 3rd millennium BC to the 20th century.

The artistic creations of the Mauryan and Gupta periods are well represented in the archaeology galleries, which display sculptures in stone, bronze and terracotta from the 3rd century BC to the 19th century AD, while the section on Buddhist art has relics of the Buddha (4th to 5th centuries BC), as well as some arresting compositions in stone, bronze, terracotta and wood. There are also scrolls called *thankas* from the neighbouring countries of Nepal and Tibet, and parts of Central Asia, which depict the three main forms of Buddhism—Hinayana, Mahayana and Vajrayana. Southern India comes alive with religious symbols and idols such as the Hindu god Shiva, the destroyer and the re-creator of the pantheon, depicted artistically in bronze.

The first floor has a superb collection of miniature paintings belonging to the Mughal and Rajasthani schools among others, which date from the 11th to the 19th centuries. Showcasing the unique variety in this art form are creations on palm leaf, wood and leather as well as southern Tanjore paintings, which are highly decorative glass paintings created with beaten gold leaf and semi-precious stones. Rounding off the memorable display on the first floor is the section on Central Asian antiquities, which is a motley combination of wall paintings, terracotta, wooden sculptures, porcelain and coins excavated by British adventurer Sir Aurel Stein during explorations in Asia in the early 20th century. The second floor has a large display of folk and classical musical instruments besides one of the finest collections of arms and ammunition used by the Mughals, Marathas, Rajputs and Sikhs in medieval India. The museum also has its own conservation laboratory and an education institute where students can take courses in the history of art, museology and conservation.

NEHRU MEMORIAL MUSEUM,
LIBRARY **AND** PLANETARIUM

The Nehru family is likened to a political dynasty in India, having produced three prime ministers who together have ruled the country for more than 35 years since independence in 1947. This illustrious first family of Indian political life came into the limelight with Motilal Nehru, a renowned lawyer and freedom fighter during the days of British colonial rule. However, it was his son Jawaharlal who took the Nehru name to the pinnacle of Indian polity and the Congress Party that was at the forefront of the freedom movement.

Jawaharlal was the political heir of Mahatma Gandhi and the first prime minister of independent India. He was succeeded by his daughter Indira Gandhi who in turn was succeeded by her son Rajiv Gandhi. Both Indira and Rajiv were assassinated. The Nehru clan is now represented by Rajiv's widow, the Italian-born Sonia, who is the president of the Congress Party, her son Rahul who is a member of parliament and her daughter Priyanka.

Jawaharlal Nehru's legacy lives on in Teen Murti House, his official residence that is closely associated with his political and personal life. The mansion, located south of the presidential palace Rashtrapati Bhavan, was originally the home of the British Commander-in chief of India and was then known as Flagstaff House. This colonial mansion, designed by British architect Robert Tor Russell and constructed in 1929-30, was renamed Teen Murti House after the Teen Murti memorial standing on the roundabout outside. The Teen Murti, or three statues memorial, is dedicated to the Indian soldiers who died in World War l.

Teen Murti House was formally inaugurated as a museum six months after Nehru's death of a heart attack on 27 May 1964. Visitors to the museum can get a first-hand look at Nehru's personal chambers, with his bedroom, drawing room and study on display, preserved in their original state. Nehru's office at the Ministry of External Affairs has been recreated at Teen Murti House and holds all the furniture and other items he had used there until his death.

The exhibit includes manuscripts, copies of his will in all languages, rare photographs and the umpteen gifts he received from visitors and during his official travels overseas. Located

Jawaharal Nehru's personal chambers at Teen Murti House such as his study, office and bedroom have been preserved in their original state.

LOCATION:
Teen Murti House, Teen Murti Road, near Chanakyapuri Diplomatic Enclave.
Tel: 23016734
Website:
http://www.nehru planetarium.org/
Closed on Monday

एक ऐतिहासिक वार्तालाप
के कुछ अंश

श्रीमती इंदिरा गांधी : भावनगर मीटर रहेगा
शर्मा, सारे राष्ट्र का ध्यान आपकी तरफ लगा है ... और हम
सब आपको बधाई देते हैं ... मैं तो आपसे बहुत से
प्रश्न पूछने में लोभ भी रोक नहीं पा रही हूँ ... अभ मैं खाली
कुछ ही पूछना चाहती हूँ ...

स्क्वाड्रन लीडर राकेश शर्मा : जी हाँ और
किसी तरह के रोक बंदेश न कि यो जहा रहा है।

श्रीमती इंदिरा गांधी : राकेश

**EXCERPTS FROM A
HISTORIC CONVERSATION**

Smt Indira Gandhi : Sqn.Ldr. Rakesh
Sharma, the attention of the entire nation
is focused on you ...Our greetings to
you...I would like to ask many questions to
, but shall restrict myself to a few. How
does our country appear to you from the
space above ?

Sqn.Ldr Rakesh sharma : Without
moment's hesitation I can say "Sare

An exhibit at the Nehru Planetarium located in Teen Murti House.

in the western wing of the building is the library, a goldmine of books in Indian and foreign languages, pamphlets, old newspapers and periodicals that go back to the early 19th century. There is extensive material available on the freedom movement and Nehru's Congress Party. Today, Teen Murti House is renowned for its museum of Nehru mementoes as well as this research library, one of the finest resource centres of modern Indian history.

On the front lawn of Teen Murti House lies a granite rock inscribed with Nehru's historic 'Tryst with Destiny' speech, made to the Indian Constituent Assembly on the eve of India's independence, at midnight on 14 August 1947. At the back of the building is Kushak Mahal, a 14th century hunting lodge built on a mound during the reign of Firoz Shah Tughlaq (r.1351-1388).

The Teen Murti House complex also houses the Nehru Planetarium, established to propagate Nehru's ideas on the importance of science in the development of children. The Planetarium has an exhibit area where the Soyuz space module, which carried India's first cosmonaut Rakesh Sharma to space in April 1984, is displayed along with his space suit and mission journal. Taped and live shows on astronomy are held at the Planetarium's sky theatre.

NIZAMUDDIN'S SHRINE

This holy Muslim site is the mausoleum of highly venerated 13th century Sufi saint Shaikh Hazrat Nizamuddin Aulia Chishti, who advocated religious tolerance and renunciation and was popular with devotees of all religious faiths. Sufis are Islamic mystics. Nizamuddin's Shrine or *dargah* as it is known locally, is a renowned pilgrimage spot which receives throngs of devotees especially during the Urs festival, held in November or December every year to mark the saint's death anniversary. Urs is an annual celebration of the death of a Sufi saint and is marked by prayer, offerings of flowers and sweets, and singing of mystical hymns called *qawwalis*. The shrine also draws hordes of devotees at sunset every Thursday when *fatiha* or prayers for the saint are offered after which *qawwali* singers sing Urdu hymns in his praise.

Nizamuddin (1236-1325) was the fourth in line of Chishti saints, a Muslim sect founded by Khwaja Muin-ud-din Chishti of Ajmer. His shrine stands in the midst of teeming narrow lanes brimming over with houses, shops and a cluster of historic monuments in Nizamuddin, once an urban village which has grown into a sprawling residential colony split into two parts, Nizamuddin East and West, in south Delhi. Many of these historic structures are tombs of members of Delhi's ruling dynasties who wished to have their final resting place in the sacred environs surrounding Nizamuddin's grave. Buried in the area are Mughal Emperor Muhammad Shah (r.1719-1748), Mughal Emperor Shah Jahan's eldest and favourite daughter Jahanara, and renowned poets Mirza Asadullah Baig Khan, or Ghalib, and Amir Khusro among others.

Chausath Khamba (meaning 64 pillars) is conspicuous because of the 64 pillars supporting its roof that it is named after. This white marble tomb belongs to Mirza Aziz Kokaltash, the son of Atgah Khan, who was chancellor in the court of Mughal Emperor Akbar. Atgah Khan's tomb is another striking structure built in red sandstone with marble and coloured tiles that allude to its original splendour. The Ghalib Academy and tomb, established in memory of the illustrious 19th century Urdu poet Mirza Ghalib, is located next to Chausath Khamba (see Mirza Ghalib, page 100). The tomb of Amir Khusro, a 13th

LOCATION:
Nizamuddin West, off Mathura Road.
Nearest Metro Station: Pragati Maidan

century Sufi poet and the most famous disciple of Nizamuddin, lies behind the tombs of Jahanara and Muhammad Shah. An Urs festival is held at the Nizamuddin Shrine every year, 16 days after Id-ul-Fitr, to mark the death anniversary of Amir Khusro.

Nizamuddin's Shrine stands in a small marble-paved courtyard, his cenotaph draped with a green cloth. The original building has been enhanced several times with arches, marble screens and pillars, and a wooden canopy with mother-of-pearl inlay. The shrine complex also holds the *baoli* or step well built by Nizamuddin which, according to legend, became a bone of contention between him and Tughlaq Emperor Ghiyas ud-din Tughlaq. The water in the baoli is said to have healing powers (see Tughlaqabad Fort, page 156).

West of the tomb lies the Jamaat Khana mosque or Khizri mosque, a unique Indo-Islamic structure that is a legacy of the Khilji and Tughlaq dynasties. The central chamber of the mosque was built in 1325 by Khizr Khan, son of Emperor Alauddin Khilji (r.1296-1316) and the side chambers were erected in the early Tughlaq period. The tomb of Jahanara Begum stands in a marble enclosure next to the Jamaat Khana mosque. It was her wish that only grass should grow on her grave, hence her cenotaph has a patch of soil on top, for grass to grow.

Devotees throng the grounds of the mausoleum during the Urs festival.

PAAN

An exotic concoction of leaf, nut and condiments, *paan* is a traditional after-dinner digestive that is popular throughout India, including Delhi. It comes in a number of variations, sweet, plain or stuffed with tobacco, and is chewed to derive maximum pleasure from it. *Paan* is available from streetside vendors who usually operate in busy marketplaces or near restaurants. They have small kiosks that carry an assortment of jars containing an array of spices and other ingredients. The *paanwallah* (paan seller) as the vendor is called, typically will create the *paan* in front of you based on your preferences.

All over Delhi, *paan* is sold at streetside kiosks that are usually found in markets, commercial centres and near restaurants.

A *paan* is created from a betel leaf (an Indo-Malayan shrub known as Piper Betle) which is given a dash of lime paste and filled with chopped betel nuts (nut of the Areca Catechu plant) and other spices. The leaf, which has stimulating properties because of the presence of alkaloids, is then folded into a triangular shape and may be secured with a clove to hold the ingredients together. Someone keen to have a plain or *saada paan* would have a stuffing of nut accompanied by cardamom or clove, which together produce a mildly bitter taste.

For a sweet or *meetha paan*, grated coconut, honey and some fruit preserves are added to the other ingredients. This is the tastiest variation of *paan* and for some people may even take the place of dessert. The tobacco *paan* is typically made with chewable tobacco or *gutkha* combined with betel nut, making it stimulating and addictive.

While *paan* is known to have digestive properties—some also believe it to be an aphrodisiac—it has been found to be addictive and carcinogenic if taken in large quantities. The combination of tobacco and betel nut is particularly harmful and believed to be a leading cause of oral cancer among Indians. Another negative quality of *paan* is the red stain that it leaves in the mouth if consumed in excess. Besides, after chewing *saada paan*, many addicts prefer to spit out the red-coloured juice rather than consume it, which is the cause of the unsightly red blotches found in many public areas in Delhi and other Indian cities. One variation of *paan* that has gained a large following is *paan masala*, which is a powdered, ready-to-eat form of *paan*.

PALIKA BAZAAR
UNDERGROUND MARKET

One can find an assortment of the latest movies released in DVD format at this basement bazaar.

Delhi's first underground air-conditioned market, Palika Bazaar is home to about 400 stores selling everything from clothes, shoes, bags, books, jewellery, toiletries to electronic items, CDs and DVDs. Confined within an enclosed space below Connaught Place's inner circle, Palika Bazaar can be accessed from any one of its seven gates. The gates open out in to the different blocks of the inner circle and access is through an underpass. This centrally located market has the advantage of being at walking distance from the Rajiv Chowk metro station and a couple of kilometres away from the New Delhi Railway Station.

Though the market is overcrowded and poorly maintained, with littered corners being a common sight, its air-conditioned ambience makes for a comfortable shopping experience in Delhi's gruelling summer heat. But as in other parts of Connaught Place, shoppers need to be prepared for haggling with shopkeepers if they want to ensure they get a good deal on their purchase. Besides the stores with their diverse range of products, Palika also has a number of food outlets where tired shoppers can stop by for a cold drink or a bite to eat.

Palika Bazaar, which created a stir because of its subterranean ambience when it opened its doors in the late 1970s, has become a favourite haunt for both locals and tourists looking for pirated DVDs of Indian and foreign movies. Pornographic discs are also available, and despite regular police raids, the illicit sale continues. However, security is a concern in this market where women have complained of harassment by the sales staff and unsavoury customers. Palika Bazaar was in the news in April 2007 for a rape case. The incident, in which a 23-year-old woman was raped by two salesmen in the late morning, highlighted the lax security in the bazaar where there are only 14 home guards on duty at any given time.

LOCATION:
Inner Circle, Connaught Place. Closed on Sunday. Nearest Metro Station: Rajiv Chowk

PRAGATI MAIDAN

Pragati Maidan is a massive exhibition complex that is a beehive of activity throughout the year. While it holds a number of national and international conferences and exhibitions in its 60.3-hectare grounds, Pragati Maidan is best known for its annual India International Trade Fair, India's largest trade fair held in November every year, and the World Book Fair. This world class exhibition complex is managed by the India Trade Promotion Organisation, the Indian government's apex trade promotion agency. It was designed by eminent architects such as Raj Rewal, Charles Correa and Satish Grover and opened in 1982, just before the Asian Games.

Located east of Connaught Place on Mathura Road, the all-purpose Pragati Maidan has exhibition halls and conference rooms, auditoriums, warehouses, restaurants as well as an amusement park, a museum and the National Science Centre. This exhibition facility offers 62,650 sq. m of covered exhibition space in 17 halls, besides 10,000 sq. m of open display area. The

LOCATION:

At the junction of Mathura Road and Bhairon Road. Nearest Metro Station: Pragati Maidan exhibition halls include the Hall of Technology, Hall of States, Hall of Nations, Hall of Special Displays and Hall of Industries, while there are special pavilions for defence and handloom products. Among the restaurants there are Phoolwari and Vatika, and the theatres include Shakuntalam and Falaknuma, both popular with the public.

So vast is Pragati Maidan that visitors need to use the shuttle service available to proceed from one gate to another. Located at Gate 1 are the Crafts Museum and the National Science Centre, while Gates 2 and 3 provide access to the various exhibition halls, restaurants and auditoriums.

Crafts Museum

This massive exhibition facility has special pavilions, halls, restaurants and theatres.

India's fascinating crafts tradition is on full display at the state-owned Crafts Museum, a conglomerate of galleries that showcase the best of wood carvings, terracotta pots, bronzes, puppets, lamps, jewellery, textiles, *saris* and metalwork from different states and from different periods of Indian history. The Gallery of Courtly Crafts has quaint bullock carts and the interior of a 19th century Gujarat mansion on display. Of particular interest is the village complex with its mud huts complete with painted walls and thatched roofs depicting styles from different regions. Visitors can also see craftsmen at work in live demonstrations of their handiwork.

National Science Centre

This is one of the biggest science centres in India and one of a chain of 27 centres run by the National Council of Science Museums in the country. The National Science Centre in Delhi has scientific models, instruments and demonstrations, such as the energy ball which shows the conversion of energy, that are designed to make science fun for children. The centre is divided into different galleries such as the Biology Gallery, where models concerning the different parts of the human body are displayed. The Dinosaur Gallery has animals from the Mesozoic period. The centre also has a planetarium, a section on India's mathematicians which explains the significant role they played in the development of mathematics in the world, and a well stocked library.

PURANA QILA (OLD FORT)

Standing adjacent to Pragati Maidan is an imposing though dilapidated 16th century monument with massive walls, three colossal gateways and a perimeter of nearly 2 km. This is Purana Qila or the Old Fort. It has an interesting history, with the foundation and initial construction carried out by Mughal emperor Humayun, but its completion being seen to by Afghan leader Sher Shah who ousted Humayun from power.

While Purana Qila is a Mughal era monument, it is significant for another reason too. The fort is located at the historic site of

LOCATION:

Mathura Road.
Tel: 24355387
Nearest Metro
Station: Pragati
Maidan

Indraprastha, a city that dates back to 1000 BC and is mentioned in the Hindu epic *Mahabharata* as the city the Pandava brothers founded next to the Yamuna River. Archaeological excavations carried out at the Purana Qila site have yielded remains of painted grey pottery that establish the existence of Indraprastha there. This theory is further reinforced by the presence of the village Indrapat, which existed in the area until 1913.

Humayun began building the fort in 1538, to be part of his city Dinpanah, but he was ousted from power by Afghan noble Sher Shah the following year. Sher Shah renamed the city Shergarh and went ahead and completed the fort, building a pavilion called the Sher Mandal, and a mosque, Qila-i-Kuhna Masjid, believed to be the best architectural work of his reign, within the complex.

The walls of Purana Qila are 18 metres high in some places, interspersed throughout by holes designed as nesting places for birds, which continue to be used for this purpose even today. There are three imposing gates—Humayun Darwaza, Talaqi Darwaza and Bara Darwaza, with the latter being the main entrance to the fort. The gates combine Hindu and Islamic architectural features with their pointed arches and decorative canopies or *chhatris*.

The most striking structure in the entire Purana Qila complex is the Qila-i-Kuhna Masjid, built in marble and sandstone by Sher Shah in 1541. The mosque, recognised as a remarkable monument for its beauty and workmanship, and a noteworthy example of Indo-Islamic architecture, has bracketed openings, archways and extensive marble inlay work, with the most significant features being the combination of marble and sandstone used at the centre of its façade, and its entrance arch of sandstone and white and black marble.

The Sher Mandal is a two-storeyed sandstone structure that has an appealing octagonal design. However, historically it is associated with the death of Humayun. This building built by Sher Shah was used as a library by Humayun on his return to the Mughal throne in 1555. A few months later, while descending the steep stairs of the Sher Mandal, Humayun slipped and fell to his death.

Visitors to Purana Qila can watch a sound and light show organised by Delhi Tourism in the evenings to get an insight into the events related to this Mughal-era fort. Tourists can also take a paddle boat ride in the moat accessed from the fourth gate or visit the Delhi Zoo which is adjacent to the Purana Qila.

QUTB MINAR

The site of Delhi's first city Lal Kot, Mehrauli, is best known for the Qutb Minar, the towering 13th century edifice that is a symbol of the first Islamic dynasty to rule India. The Qutb Minar stands in a historically rich complex that includes the Quwwat-ul-Islam Mosque, Alai Darwaza, Alai Minar, Tomb of Iltutmish, Imam Zamin's Tomb and the Iron Pillar. The Iron Pillar is the oldest of these monuments, having been built in the 4th century while the rest of the buildings, significant examples of early Islamic architecture, were erected in the 12th to 16th centuries.

The Qutb Minar is a 13th century monument that is a symbol of the first Islamic dynasty that ruled India.

The pride of place in the Qutb Complex goes to the Qutb Minar (meaning axis minaret), a 72.5-metre high monument that measures over 14 metres at its base and about 3 metres at its tip. This tower, akin to Afghan victory towers, was built by the first sultan of Delhi, Qutb-ud-din Aibak (r.1206-1210), and his successor Iltutmish, both of whom belonged to the Slave dynasty which established Islamic rule in India in 1206. The five-storey tower, created with sandstone and marble, has angular and circular flutings and projecting balconies that add to the beauty of its harmonious design.

Qutb-ud-din Aibak was able to build only the first storey of the tower, using sandstone as his building material. It was completed by his son-in-law and successor Iltutmish (r.1210-35) who built three more storeys. In the 14th century, during Firoz Shah Tughlaq's reign, the tower was damaged by lightning and reconstructed. Firoz Shah, who had a passion for buildings, replaced the top storey with two more, using marble for the construction. He then surmounted the structure with a harp-shaped cupola.

The British made their contribution to the tower in 1828, when they added parapets to the balconies and replaced the cupola after it suffered damage in an earthquake. The re-created cupola, which appeared strangely out of place on the tower, was later shifted to the gardens of the Qutb complex. It is referred to as Smith's Folly, for the part British engineer Major Robert Smith played in its creation.

The Alai Minar, a rubble structure to the north of the Qutb Minar, was Emperor Alauddin Khilji's (r.1296 to 1316) unfinished attempt at creating a tower that was taller and more

LOCATION:

Qutb Complex,
Aurobindo Marg,
Mehrauli, south
Delhi

majestic than the Qutb Minar. However, he died before the monument could be completed and it was left in its unfinished state at a height of about 24.5 metres. Alauddin Khilji did complete the ornate Alai Darwaza, a domed gateway built in 1311 that is acclaimed for its magnificent Indo-Islamic design.

Created with latticed stone screens and inscriptions from the holy Qur'an, the sandstone-and-marble Alai Darwaza is the southern gateway to the Quwwat-ul-Islam (Might of Islam) Mosque, the first Islamic place of worship to be built in Delhi. Next to the mosque stands Imam Zamin's Tomb, a 16th century mausoleum built by Imam Zamin, a functionary of the mosque. Qutb-ud-din, who was a pious Muslim nicknamed 'Lakh Baksh' or 'giver of hundred thousands' for his generous nature, built the grandly embellished Quwwat-ul-Islam Mosque with ornamental pillars carved with Hindu motifs of bells and garlands, believed to have been obtained from 27 Hindu temples. Alauddin later extended the mosque.

The Iron Pillar in the courtyard of the Quwwat-ul-Islam Mosque is a metallurgical curiosity, having withstood corrosion since it was built during the reign of Chandragupta ll (r.380-415 AD). Its unusually good resistance to corrosion appears to be due to a high content of phosphorus. The pillar is almost 7 metres high and has an idol of the mythical bird Garuda on top. It was originally located at a place called Vishnupadagiri near present-day Bhopal, Madhya Pradesh, and was brought to Delhi. Standing to the west of the Quwwat-ul-Islam Mosque is the remarkable tomb of Iltutmish, built by Iltutmish himself in 1235. The distinguishing feature of this mausoleum is the elaborate carving throughout its interior. These embellishments are inscriptions from the holy Qur'an.

RANG DE **BASANTI**

Delhi has made it to the silver screen numerous times, being the location of choice for Bollywood filmmakers keen to capitalise on the city's unique history and ethos. This ethos was especially on display in the 2006 award-winning Bollywood blockbuster *Rang De Basanti*, directed by Rakeysh Omprakash Mehra and featuring Hindi star Aamir Khan, British actress Alice Patten and Hindi actress Soha Ali Khan. *Rang De Basanti* (Paint It Saffron) was India's entry in the Best Foreign Film category for the US Academy Awards but did not make it to the short list of nominees. However, the film won the prestigious Best Film honour at the 2007 International Indian Film Academy Awards, Bollywood's Oscars, in June 2007, besides several other top Indian awards, such as the Filmfare and Zee Best Film and Best Director trophies.

Rang De Basanti, a contemporary Hindi-language drama which harks back to British colonial days, tells the story of a young British girl Sue McKinley who arrives in Delhi to make a documentary drama on the freedom struggle. She is inspired to make the movie after reading the diaries of her grandfather, who was a police officer in British-ruled India. Sue takes the help of her friend, Sonia, a student at Delhi University, to recruit DJ, the lead role played by Aamir Khan and some of his friends to act in the movie. The character of Sue is played by Alice Patten, the daughter of Chris Patten, the last British governor of Hong Kong.

Delhi has also played host to the crew of other big budget Bollywood films such as *Fanaa* starring Aamir Khan and Kajol, the Amitabh Bachchan starrer *Cheeni Kum*, *Chak De India* with superstar Shah Rukh Khan, *Mera Bharat Mahaan* with Sanjay Dutt and Salman Khan and the small budget films *Khosla Ka Ghosla* and *Delhi Heights*.

What has attracted filmmakers to shoot in outdoor locations in the Indian capital are its many monuments built during the Mughal period, which give it an appealing old-world charm; its wide open spaces and broad tree-lined avenues, specially in Lutyens' New Delhi; and its seasonal climate unlike Mumbai, the home of Bollywood, where there is little variation and it is warm and humid most of the year. In the case of *Chak De India*, which revolves around hockey, the National Stadium in the Indian capital was a particular draw. The Film City in Delhi's satellite town Noida is also popular with Bollywood filmmakers because of its well-equipped studios and scenic outdoor locales (see Gurgaon and Noida, page 58).

Following the tremendous success of *Rang De Basanti*, its director Rakeyesh Omprakash Mehra is planning to film his next venture *Dilli 6* in Delhi too. This time around, he will focus on old Delhi, specifically the teeming area of Chandni Chowk, one of the oldest and busiest markets of Delhi that was at the heart of Shajahanabad, the city Mughal Emperor Shah Jahan established as his capital in the 17th century.

Aamir Khan, the lead actor in *Rang De Basanti* poses with a marketing premium made for the movie.

RASHTRAPATI BHAVAN

Rashtrapati Bhavan or the Presidential Palace is unsurpassed among Delhi's colonial buildings in size and grandeur. Designed to be the residence of the British Viceroy, it was meant to represent the power of the British Empire in stone, hence the splendour of its design and workmanship, and its location on Raisina Hill at the centre of Lutyens' New Delhi. However, the edifice took 17 years to build, instead of the expected four, and was completed in 1929. The Viceroy's House was renamed Government House when India became independent in 1947, and Rashtrapati Bhavan on 26 January 1950 when it became the official residence of Dr Rajendra Prasad, the first President of India.

The Jaipur Column soaring 44 metres high and topped by a six-pointed glass star is one of the distinctive features of Rashtrapati Bhavan.

Rashtrapati Bhavan, which is bounded by the two Secretariat office blocks and Sansad Bhavan or Parliament House, has a floor area of 18,581 sq. m. The reception rooms are in the central block while private rooms and offices are located in the wings. It has 340 rooms, with the marble and golden-pillared Durbar Hall, the ceremonial hall situated beneath the dome where all major official functions are held, being the most resplendent. The Ashoka Hall, designed as the state ballroom, is also ornate with a painted ceiling that depicts a royal hunting expedition. The Yellow Drawing Room is used for less important state functions such as the swearing-in of a minister into the Council of Ministers.

Rashtrapati Bhavan's most distinctive feature is its dome, believed to have been inspired by the pantheon in Rome as well as the Buddhist stupa at Sanchi. Other features include the Mughal Gardens at the back and a large forecourt with its 44-metre high Jaipur Column, a gift from the Maharajah of the princely state of Jaipur. This column made of red sandstone is topped by a striking bronze lotus flower with a six-pointed glass star soaring from it. Completing the president's estate, spread over a total area of 143.3 hectares, is a polo ground, a cricket field, a 14-hole golf course and nine tennis courts.

As many as 700 million bricks and 85,000 cubic metres of sandstone, in red and cream colour, were used in the construction of the Rashtrapati Bhavan. Edwin Lutyens was the chief architect of the project while the chief engineer was Hugh Keeling, and the contractors included Haroun-al-Rashid and the father-and-son duo of Sujan and Sobha Singh. In designing

LOCATION:

Raisina Hill, at western end of Rajpath. http:// presidentofindia. nic.in/ Nearest Metro Station: Central Secretariat.

Rashtrapati Bhavan, Lutyens combined Indian and European elements in an impressive fusion of styles. He blended Indian elements, such as temple bells, massive columns, verandahs, arches, canopies or *chhatris, jalis* or decorative stone screens and *chajjas* or broad eaves, with classical European architecture.

While the Rashtrapati Bhavan is not open to the general public, certain sections such as the Durbar Hall, which was known as the Throne Room during British rule, the Ashoka Hall and the Dining or Banquet Hall which can seat 104 people, can be seen with special permission from the President's office. The Mughal Gardens are open to the public only in the spring period of February to March every year when the flowers are in full bloom. The changing of the guard ceremony at Rashtrapati Bhavan can be viewed every Saturday morning.

> The Presidential Palace is not open to the public though certain sections can be accessed with special permission.

Mughal Gardens

The Mughal Gardens at Rashtrapati Bhavan are spread across six hectares and comprise three sections—the Main Garden, the Long Garden and Circular Garden—that cascade onto each other in the typical Mughal terraced design. The gardens, which creatively combine Mughal and Victorian features, were designed by Edwin Lutyens, chief architect of Delhi, in collaboration with WR Mustoe of the Horticultural Department. They were created at the behest of Baroness Hardinge, wife of Charles Hardinge, the British viceroy of India from 1910 to 1916, and were ready by 1929. Lutyens is believed to have drawn inspiration for the gardens from Persian miniature paintings as well as the majestic gardens created by the Mughal emperors in Kashmir and other parts of the country.

Luxuriant flowerbeds spill onto manicured lawns, sporting over 250 varieties of roses, 60 varieties of bougainvillea, 18-inch-wide dahlias in different hues, gerbera, lineria, viola, pansy, calendula, larkspur, gaznia, viscaria, oxalis, 13 varieties of Indian marigold and a host of other exotic flower species.

Other attractions include the Cactus Corner, Spiritual Garden which has trees and shrubs from religious texts and the Herbal Garden with its assortment of medicinal plants.

REPUBLIC DAY **PARADE**

India proudly celebrated its newfound status as a sovereign democratic republic on 26 January 1950 with a parade in Delhi, commanded by Brig Joginder Singh Dhillon and held at the Irwin Stadium (present-day National Stadium). Since then, annual parades and flag ceremonies have been held across the country on 26 January. The most magnificent parade is the one held in Delhi, which has grown from a meticulous display by the contingents of the Army, Navy, Air Force and the Police, to a spectacular cultural feast watched by millions on live television. The two-hour-long parade takes place in central Delhi, along a route that extends from the Rashtrapati Bhavan presidential palace down through the broad tree-lined avenue Rajpath, past India Gate after which it snakes its way through Connaught Place to its final destination, the Red Fort in old Delhi. Spectator enclosures are erected along the route while the VIP galleries are located on Rajpath, near India Gate.

In a ceremonial start to the annual Republic Day celebrations, the Prime Minister of India lays a wreath at the Amar Jawan Jyoti memorial to the unknown soldier at India Gate (see India Gate and the Amar Jawan Jyoti, page 66) before the President, who holds the title of the Supreme Commander of the Armed

The plaza beneath the Secretairat Buildings is the venue of the Beating the Retreat ceremony that marks the end of the Republic Day festivities.

LOCATION:

Republic Day Parade held on January 26 on Rajpath; Beating the Retreat held on January 29 at Vijay Chowk. Nearest Metro Station: Central Secretariat.

Forces, arrives with the chief guest, usually a visiting foreign head of state.

The parade begins with the defence forces segment, which includes a display of everything from tanks, missiles and guns to a marchpast of the forces and the magnificent horses of the cavalry regiment. The cultural segment features picturesque folk dances besides colourful tableaux on floats from diverse Indian states, each showcasing the unique arts, crafts, history and traditions of that particular region. A highlight of the parade is the pageant by children, with the recepients of the National Bravery Awards, mounted on elephants, evoking the maximum applause from the hundreds and thousands of spectators. A dramatic flypast by the Indian Air Force concludes the splendid presentation.

The formal closing of the Republic Day festivities actually takes place three days later, on the evening of 29 January, with the Beating The Retreat, a rousing performance by the 20 bands of the Army, Navy and Air Force. This solemn ceremony is held at Vijay Chowk (Victory Square), the plaza between the Secretariat Buildings, at the west end of Rajpath. The bands take turns to play traditional Scottish and Indian tunes, before winding up with a stirring rendition of the Christian hymn *Abide With Me*. A bugle call signals the retreat of the bands, which march away towards Raisina Hill playing the energetic Indian patriotic song *Sare Jahan Se Accha*.

SANSAD BHAVAN

Built in red and cream sandstone like Rashtrapati Bhavan, Sansad Bhavan or Parliament House is a circular colonnaded building that lies at the end of Sansad Marg, north of Rajpath. It was built almost as an afterthought a few years after the original layout of New Delhi had been conceived, hence its rather obscure location compared to the other government buildings in Lutyens' imperial capital. It was because of the Montagu-Chelmsford reforms of 1919, which enhanced Indian participation in government, that it became necessary to build a separate parliament house—the original plan was to allocate an area for parliament in Rashtrapati Bhavan.

India's lawmakers discuss issues of national interest in this circular building designed by British architect Herbert Baker.

Sansad Bhavan, 114 metres in diameter and 22.8 metres high, consists of a circular central hall surmounted by a dome and three semi-circular chambers that are linked to the central chamber via lobbies. Offices are located outside the chambers and a continuous 144-column verandah stretches right around the entire building. The boundary wall, which encloses Sansad Bhavan, is made of Mughal-style sandstone-screens or *jalis*.

Sansad Bhavan was designed by Lutyens' associate Herbert Baker, though the idea to make it circular came from Lutyens. Baker had to create separate structures so that the Council of State, the Legislative Assembly and the Chamber of Princes could all exist under one roof. The building, completed in 1927 and originally known as the Council Chamber, today is home to the two houses of Parliament, the *Lok Sabha* (Lower House or House of the People) and the *Rajya Sabha* (Upper House or Council of States), and a library.

The august Central Hall is used for combined sittings of both houses. It has also been the venue for numerous historic events such as the official British handover of power to a free India on 15 August 1947. Its oak-panelled walls are lined with portraits of the nationalists who helped create independent India. For security reasons, visitors to Sansad Bhavan, whether Parliament is in session or not, need a special permit available from the visitor's reception office on nearby Raisina Road. Foreign nationals need to apply for a pass through their high commission/embassy. All visitors to the parliamentary library also need an official permit.

LOCATION:

At the junction of Talkatora Road and Parliament Street. Nearest Metro Station: Central Secretariat

SECRETARIAT BUILDINGS

Completing the magnificent vista at Rajpath or Kingsway in Lutyens' Delhi are the Secretariat Buildings, comprising the north and south blocks. The Indian government is using these buildings to house some of its principal offices, with the South Block occupied by the Prime Minister's Office, the Ministry of Defence and the Ministry of External Affairs, and the North Block in use by the Ministry of Finance and the Ministry of Home. A visitor's pass is needed to enter these buildings.

The Secretariat Buildings, a legacy of British architect Herbert Baker, are located on Raisina Hill, just before it slopes downwards towards the stately Rashtrapati Bhavan presidential palace. The two buildings are built in sandstone, in tune with the other imposing structures of the British Raj in the area. They are

LOCATION:
Raisina Hill, at western end of Rajpath. Nearest Metro Station: Central Secretariat

Built of sandstone, the British-era Secretariat Buildings present a blend of classical Western and Indian architecture.

a blend of classic Western and Indian architecture, with liberal use of colonnades, domes, ornamental screens or *jalis*, canopies known as *chhatris* and broad eaves or *chajjas*. Inside, there are vaulted staircases, high ceilings and long corridors. Each building has its own entrance, and between these stand the four Dominion columns. These sandstone columns, each crowned by a bronze ship sailing east, were donated by Australia, Canada, New Zealand and South Africa and represented the four dominions of the British Empire at that time.

The buildings also have the foundation stones of New Delhi laid by British monarch George V and Queen Mary at the 1911 Durbar held at the Coronation Memorial Park in north Delhi, where the transfer of the administrative headquarters of the British from Calcutta to Delhi was announced. The stones were moved to the Secretariat during the construction of the two buildings, after the plan to centre the British capital in the Coronation Memorial area was abandoned.

The plaza at the base of the slope between the two buildings is called Vijay Chowk (Victory Square), formerly known as Central Vista. It is here that the ceremonial Beating the Retreat ceremony takes place on 29 January every year, three days after the Republic Day parade held on Rajpath.

The building of the Secretariat and the road leading up to it proved to be a major bone of contention between Edwin Lutyens and Baker, close collaborators in the building of New Delhi. Their differences came to be known as the "Battle of the Gradient". The dispute was centred on the gradient of Raisina Hill with Lutyens keen to change it so that the Viceroy's House, now Rashtrapati Bhavan, would be at a higher level than the Secretariat buildings and therefore clearly visible from a long distance. Baker, on the other hand, proposed to keep the existing gradient, a view shared by the Viceroy Charles Hardinge, so that all three buildings would be at the same level. The friendship between the two men ended because of the dispute and was never revived. The two refused to talk to each other until their respective deaths, Lutyens' in 1944 and Baker's in 1946.

The Indian government uses both the North Block and South Block for its principal offices.

SEVEN CITIES OF DELHI

Delhi has a chequered history dating back to 1000 BC, and has been built and rebuilt umpteen times by the disparate dynasties that have made it the pivot of their mighty empires in India. Archaeological remains point to Delhi being the site of the city of Indraprastha (meaning abode of the King of the Gods), the capital of the legendary Pandava brothers, whose mighty battle against their cousins, the Kauravas, was detailed in the revered Hindu epic *Mahabharata* (see Purana Qila, page 122). The epic talks about the site being a jungle until the Pandavas built their city there.

According to historical records, the name Delhi comes from King Dhilu who ruled the area in 600 AD. However, it was many centuries later, under the Rajput warriors, that the area came into prominence and became a major centre of power in the country. By the 12th century, the Delhi region became a prime target of Muslim invaders attracted by its wealth and pre-eminence.

Historians refer to the seven cities of Delhi to explain the seven different command centres that were established here from the 11th century until the 17th century, before the British built their imperial capital New Delhi in the 20th century. These seven cities are Lal Kot-Qila Rai Pithora; Siri; Tughlaqabad; Jahanpanah; Firozabad; Dinapanah-Shergarh-Purana Qila and Shahjahanabad. Each city has left a rich legacy of tombs, forts, palaces and other buildings, most of them in ruins, which have cemented the extraordinary ethos of Delhi.

Lal Kot-Qila Rai Pithora

Lal Kot was the name of the fortress built by Anang Pal II of the Tomar clan of the Rajputs, Hindu warriors who came into prominence in the 7th century in north-western and central India. Lal Kot was constructed in the mid 11th century and the Tomars later built temples around the fort as a small settlement took shape in the Mehrauli area of present-day Delhi. About a century later, the Tomars were defeated by the Chauhans, another clan of the Rajputs, who went on to rename the area Qila Rai Pithora after their leader Prithviraj Chauhan, and developed it into an important Hindu centre. Large parts of Qila Rai Pithora were destroyed by Muslim invader Muhammad of Ghur after he defeated Prithviraj Chauhan and captured Delhi in 1192.

Siri

Delhi's second city is Siri, built in the 14th century by Alauddin Khilji at the site of an army camping ground that stood in the vicinity of present-day Hauz Khas. This was the first city built by Muslim rulers of the Delhi Sultanate, the kingdom established in Delhi by Qutb-ud-Din Aibak of the Mamluk (Slave) Dynasty. The Khilji Dynasty succeeded the Mamluk Dynasty, with first Jalal-ud-din and then his nephew Alauddin ruling the empire. Alauddin (r.1296-1316) was an arrogant king, notorious for his cruelty to Hindus, but he had a passion for buildings and established Siri during his reign. The city got its water supply from a tank which Alauddin excavated. Hauz Khas, literally meaning 'royal tank', gets its name from this tank (see Hauz Khas, page 60). The remains of Siri can be found near Siri Fort Auditorium on Khel Gaon Marg, and the adjacent Shahpur Jat Village.

Tughlaqabad

The Tughlaq Dynasty succeeded the Khiljis in 1320, and to fortify his kingdom from the constant threat of invasions from the Mongols of Central Asia, Ghiyas ud-din Tughlaq built the city of Tughlaqabad, and within it his palace and the indomitable Tughlaqabad Fort, 8 km east of Siri on the outskirts of present-day Delhi. But Ghiyas ud-din died suddenly in 1325 in an accident believed to have been engineered by his son Muhammad bin Tughlaq who succeeded him to the throne. Tughlaqabad was abandoned shortly after Ghiyas ud-din's death and lies in ruins today. (See Tughlaqabad Fort, page 156)

Jahanpanah

Muhammad bin Tughlaq (r.1325-1351) was responsible for building Delhi's fourth city Jahanpanah between 1326 to 1327. The 44-domed Begumpuri Masjid, with its *madrasa* or school, treasury and a meeting place, was the nucleus of the city created by joining Siri and Lal Kot with two walls. Close to it stood the Bijay Mandal palace. Muhammad bin Tughlaq expanded his kingdom deep into the south and transferred his capital from Delhi to the southern city of Devagiri, renamed Daulatabad, but moved it back in two years for lack of facilities at Devagiri. The remains of Jahanpanah are visible around Khirki village, near the Malviya Nagar area of south Delhi.

Firozabad

Muhammad bin Tughlaq died in 1351 of illness and it was his successor, his cousin Firoz Shah (r.1351-1388), who established the fifth city Firozabad, named after himself, in 1354. Under Firoz Shah, power shifted to present-day central Delhi where he located his citadel, Firoz Shah Kotla, on the banks of the Yamuna River. The city rapidly grew in wealth and influence, stretching all the way from Hauz Khas to the banks of the Yamuna River.

Dinpanah-Shergarh-Purana Qila

After Mughal Emperor Humayun (r.1530-39, 1555-56) came to power, he began to build his fort and city of Dinpanah (Asylum of Faith) near Firoz Shah Kotla. However, his reign was unexpectedly shortlived and he was ousted by Afghan noble Sher Shah in 1539 before he could complete construction. Sher Shah renamed Dinpanah as Shergarh and completed work on the fort, later called Purana Qila, from which he ruled the city. Humayun regained control of the empire in 1555 but died six months later from a fall down the steep steps of his library, the two-storeyed building Sher Mandal, in the Purana Qila.

Shahjahanabad

Humayun's son Akbar (r.1556-1605) moved the capital of his empire to Agra and it was only in the 17th century, under Akbar's grandson Shah Jahan (r.1627-1658), that Delhi regained prominence as the seat of Mughal power. Shah Jahan, the greatest builder of the Mughal empire, built Shahjahanabad or 'abode of Shah Jahan', commonly referred to as Delhi's seventh city, from the ruins of Firozabad and Shergarh. The city, built between 1639 and 1648, became a focal point of religion, the arts and commerce. It was a self-contained hub of activity that had 14 gates, enclosed markets or *katras*, thousands of workshops and manufacturing units, hospitals, inns, private houses or *havelis*, Mughal Emperor Shah Jahan's massive fort and palace, mosques, temples, schools, gardens, a web of narrow lanes or *galis*, and the central avenue Chandni Chowk, named after the moonlight glistening in the canal that ran down its middle. Today Shahjahanabad is referred to as old Delhi or the walled city, a dilapidated, congested section which is of vital historical and commercial value to the metropolis and its millions of residents.

SHANKAR'S INTERNATIONAL
DOLLS MUSEUM

LOCATION:
Nehru House,
4 Bahadur Shah
Zafar Marg.
Tel: 23316970-74
Website:
http://www.
childrensbooktrust.
com/dm.html
Closed on Monday.

This museum in Delhi boasts one of the largest collections of costume dolls in the world. The man behind this unique museum was a prominent political cartoonist named Keshav Shankar Pillai, popularly known as Shankar.

For Shankar, who passed away in December 1989, the idea for the museum began with a gift from the Hungarian ambassador to India in the early 1950s. The Hungarian doll was actually meant to be a prize in an art competition Shankar instituted. But Shankar liked it so much he asked to keep it for himself. That doll started his collection which grew to 500 dolls, collected from around the world during his travels abroad as part of the press delegation of then Prime Minister Jawaharlal Nehru.

The Dolls Museum came into being in 1965 with 1,000 dolls. Today there are 6,500 exhibits from almost 85 countries. The museum is divided into two sections, one for exhibits from Europe, the United States, Australia and New Zealand, and the other one for dolls from Asia, the Middle East and Africa.

An onsite workshop lets visitors see Indian costume dolls being handcrafted. These dolls, created after meticulous research into the facial expressions, mannerisms and attire of the region in India that they come from, are popular with collectors.

Displayed in long, wall-mounted cabinets, the dolls are dressed in colourful ethnic attire representative of their country of origin.

SNACKS

When it comes to snacks and savouries, there is plenty to choose from in Delhi where popular items from every region of India are available at streetside vendors, the local *mithai* shops, such as Nathu's and Haldiram Bhujiawala and even the more classy eateries and restaurants like Kwality in Connaught Place.

Indigenous to the city, and the rest of north India, are the vegetarian favourites such as *chole bhature, aloo tikki, samosa, papdi chaat, golgappa, kachori* and *namkeen*, each one deep fried and prepared with a generous dose of spices. These snacks are typically enjoyed at tea time, or they can be eaten as appetisers before the main course. *Namkeen*, like potato chips, can be bought in ready-to-eat bags from supermarkets and kept at home or in the office for a quick nibble between meals. Non-vegetarian snacks include *samosas* with meat fillings, *pakoras* made from chicken or fish, and kebabs such as *seekh kebabs* and *shammi kebabs* (see Mughlai Cuisine, page 104).

A streetside vendor frying potatoes and *aloo tikkis*.

Aloo Tikki

Aloo tikki is a patty (*tikki*) that is prepared from boiled and mashed potatoes (*aloo*). Coriander leaves, green chillies, salt and red chilly powder are added to the potato mixture which is then shaped into round patties and deep fried. The patties are served with green coriander chutney, sweet tamarind chutney, onions and the chickpeas preparation *chole*. *Aloo tikki* can also be eaten with a bun, like a burger.

Chole Bhature

This dish, originating in the northern state of Punjab, neighbouring Delhi, can be eaten as a snack or as the main course. Made of wholesome chickpeas, *chole* is a delicious vegetarian curry that is prepared with onions, garlic, ginger, tomatoes and a mixture of spices. The *bhature* is created from white flour which has been fermented with yeast. This is then rolled out into a round shape and deep fried. *Chole bhature* is eaten accompanied by pickle and onion.

Golgappa

Golgappa, called *pani puri* in Mumbai, is a spicy concoction that is messy to eat but delectable nevertheless. The *puri* (a kind of miniature hollow puff) is made from wheat flour and semolina dough and rolled out into rounds two inches in diameter. Deep frying gives it the fluffed up appearance. A hole is made in the centre of this puff, which is then filled with a combination of boiled potatoes and chickpeas, given a dash of sweet chutney and dipped in tamarind water (*pani*) before it is popped into the mouth. The water, known as *jal jeera*, is made from a combination of tamarind pulp and spices making it highly pungent. Be prepared for *jal jeera* dripping down your chin when you attempt to eat this savoury.

Kachori

Kachori is a kind of stuffed bread that is hugely popular in the northern state of Uttar Pradesh. It is created from wheat flour dough which is stuffed with a filling of potato or peas, or both. Spicy lentil is another common stuffing. The *kachori* is rolled out with the filling inside and then deep fried till it is crisp. It can be eaten as a main course or as a snack with yoghurt and chutney. It is a special favourite on festival days and is prepared as part

of the celebratory family feast. *Kachoris* are also prepared with a sweet filling that may include coconut.

Namkeen

This is a mass consumption snack that comes in a variety of options from a sweet and sour preparation, to a spicy version laden with cashews, raisins and peanuts. It is commonly prepared from puffed rice or pressed rice flakes which have been deep fried and flavoured with salt, sugar and spices. Other ingredients include gram flour, sago, lentil and spices such as cumin powder, ginger powder, mango powder and black salt. *Namkeen* is sold in a variety of flavours and by a number of companies such as Bikaner and Haldiram's. It is also sold by *mithai* (sweetmeat) shops under their own house brand.

Pakora

Onions, potatoes, spinach, cauliflower, brinjal, green chilly, a combination of mixed vegetables, or even bread slices can be used to make *pakoras*, another deep fried snack that is enjoyed throughout north India. *Pakoras* can also be prepared with cottage cheese, known as *paneer* locally, or chicken and fish, though the non-vegetarian options are not commonly available. The vegetable, bread slice or meat is usually dipped in a batter of gram flour and spices and then deep fried until it is crisp and

Snacks come in many shapes, sizes and combinations with the triangular-shaped *samosa* being a particular favourite.

golden brown. *Pakoras* make delicious appetisers and taste best served hot accompanied by sweet and sour chutneys.

Papdi Chaat

A flattened version of the *puri* in *pani puri*, *papdi* is made from refined flour and deep fried. These flat discs are clustered together on a plate and layered with yoghurt, coriander and sweet chutney and diced boiled potatoes to create *papdi chaat*. Spices such as *chaat masala* and red chilly powder are sprinkled on top to give it a pungent taste. This snack is a crowd-puller at tea parties and birthday parties and can easily be prepared at home since the main ingredient, *papdi*, is available in Indian stores in a ready-to-eat form. All that is needed to complete the dish is the addition of yoghurt, spices and chutneys.

Samosa

Vegetarian and non-vegetarian options are available in this snack which is just as delicious stuffed with pre-cooked potatoes, mixed vegetables or cottage cheese (*paneer*) as it is with cooked minced meat. It is created from a pastry sheet that has been rolled into a triangular shell, stuffed with a filling and deep fried. *Samosas* come in large and small sizes and are served with different kinds of chutneys. There are sweet versions too, made for festive occasions such as the Hindu festivals of Holi and Diwali.

ST JAMES **CHURCH**

Tucked away in a green corner of north Delhi's Kashmere Gate area stands St James Church, Delhi's oldest church. This cream and white building dating back to the 19th century, is best known for the man who established it, James Skinner, a flamboyant personality of Scottish and Indian parentage, who began his military career as an ensign in the Maratha army and eventually became a lieutenant colonel in the British army.

Skinner, referred to as 'Sikander Sahib' by the locals for his similarity to ancient Greek conqueror Alexander the Great, made a name for himself because of his irregular cavalry unit called Skinner's Horse which was later absorbed into the regular army. The members of the unit were noticeable because of their

Delhi's oldest church is an enduring symbol of James Skinner, a flamboyant personality popularly known as "Sikander Sahib".

yellow uniforms, and were renowned for their valour. In the 1930s, the horses gave way to vehicles, and it is in this way that the unit still serves the army today.

Due to his mixed parentage, his mother was a Rajput princess, Skinner was strongly influenced by Indian ways, enjoying Indian food, smoking the local pipe *hookah*, speaking Persian fluently and even writing a book in the language. He is believed to have had a large family with 14 wives, and lived like an Indian landlord with a section in his home reserved exclusively for women.

The church he built at a cost of 20,000 pounds sterling was consecrated in 1836. Skinner took a vow to construct the place of worship while he was lying badly wounded, close to death, on the battlefield at Uniara, Rajasthan in January 1800, when he was serving under the Marathas. A poor village woman saved his life and after his recovery he set about fulfilling his promise to build the church. After his death in December 1841 at the age of 63, Skinner was buried with full military honours at Hansi, Punjab, but his remains were moved to St James Church a few months later. While Skinner lies buried inside the church, the graves of his family members can be found in a cemetery near the church.

William Fraser, an agent to the governor general during the British Raj, who was later appointed Resident, was also buried in the church grounds. Visible behind the church is an imposing building with a dome that presently functions as the administrative office of the Indian Railways, but once was the home of William Fraser. Fraser also built a house in the Ridge area where he lived until his murder in 1835. This house now functions as the premises of the Hindu Rao Hospital.

Skinner's grave lies in front of the altar of the church, which has been built in a Western classical style with a Greek cross design. The central dome of the church resembles the dome designed by Filippo Brunelleschi in the Florence Cathedral in Florence, Italy. The original ball and cross of the dome was destroyed during the Sepoy Mutiny of 1857 and was later replaced with the existing one. The church has elegant stained glass windows which were added to its interior some years after it was constructed. The stained glass windows were restored during extensive conservation work carried out at the church by the Indian Trust for Art and Cultural Heritage (INTACH). St James Church holds service only on Sundays.

LOCATION:
At the intersection of Church Road and Lothian Road. Nearest Metro Station: Kashmere Gate.

SWAMINARAYAN AKSHARDHAM **TEMPLE**

It has been described as a spiritual theme park, a cultural Disneyland, an architectural marvel and one of the spiritual wonders of the modern world. With its 40.5-hectare grounds replete with sights and sounds akin to a theme park, the Akshardham Temple is more of a cultural complex than a

place of worship for Hindu devotees. This grandiose 21st century creation that stands on the banks of the Yamuna River is dedicated to the 18th century saint Bhagwan Swaminarayan. It opened its doors to the public on 8 November 2005.

What makes Akshardham different from the other temples in Delhi is its fusion of religion, culture, history, and technology to create a unique experience for anyone who visits it. Here, not only do devotees get to pay their respects to Hindu gods, they also get to take a journey through ancient Indian history to the very foundations of Hinduism. The complex comprises the main temple building, a pond filled with waters from 151 holy rivers, a musical fountain, a step well or Yagnapurush Kund, exhibition halls, an IMAX theatre, and two meditation gardens—the Bharat Upavan and the Yodi Hraday Kamal sunken garden. Tourist attractions include a 12-minute indoor boat-ride that takes you back in time to the ancient Vedic civilisation, a light and sound show, and animatronics depicting the life of Bhagwan Swaminarayan.

The 43-metre high temple building itself is a palatial structure constructed entirely of pink sandstone and white marble and completely devoid of any steel supports. It stands on a plinth decorated with 148 elephants and is designed with ornate pillars, towers and domes, with thousands of carvings of Hindu deities and motifs scattered all around. The principal idol, among the 20,000 in the temple, is a 3.4-metre high gold coated statue of Bhagwan Swaminarayan.

It took two billion rupees and the efforts of 7,000 artisans and 4,000 volunteers over five years to create this monumental complex, the fulfilment of a desire expressed by Brahmaswarup Yogiji Maharaj, the late spiritual master of the Bochasanwasi Shri Akshar Purushottam Swaminarayan Sanstha (BAPS). BAPS is a Hindu organisation established in 1907 to uphold the teachings of Bhagwan Swaminarayan. Among notable temples belonging to the organisation, which has thousands of followers around the world, are the Akshardham Temple in Gandhinagar, Gujarat and the Swaminarayan Hindu Temple in London.

LOCATION:
National Highway 24 near Noida Mor, east Delhi.
Tel: 22016688, 22026688
Website:
http://www.akshardham.com
Closed on Monday.

TUGHLAQABAD FORT

Tughlaqabad Fort was a magnificent edifice built to reflect the power and glory of the Tughlaq Dynasty in 14th century Delhi. It was the brainchild of the dynasty's first monarch, Ghiyas ud-din Tughlaq, who ascended the throne of the Delhi Sultanate in 1320 after the fall of the Khilji Dynasty (r.1290-1320). But this citadel, built to fortify Tughlaqabad, the third city of Delhi that Ghiyas ud-din built as the seat of his power, was inhabited only briefly. It was abandoned shortly after the death of Ghiyas ud-din Tughlaq in 1325. According to legend, a curse by Sufi saint Nizamuddin Auliya was the cause of the premature dereliction of what was an architectural masterpiece of that time.

As the story goes, Nizamuddin was involved in the construction of a *baoli* (step well) at the same time as Tughlaqabad Fort was being built, and he pinched many of the labourers for his own project. An angry Ghiyas ud-din forbade the labourers from working for Nizamuddin but when the work continued unabated at night, he halted the sale of oil for the lamps used by Nizamuddin. The Sufi saint eventually finished his project but not before he cursed Ghiyas ud-din saying Tughlaqabad would be inhabited only by members of the nomadic Gujar tribe. The saint had also prophesised that Ghiyas ud-din would not live to see Delhi again.

The Tughlaq monarch died the same year the fort was completed, when a temporary pavilion erected in his honour collapsed, killing him. Ghiyas ud-din's accidental death, suspected to have been engineered by his son and successor Muhammad bin Tughlaq, marked the downfall of Tughlaqabad city which was later abandoned, lending credence to Nizamuddin's prophecy and curse.

Tughlaqabad Fort stands on an outcrop of rock, a massive half hexagon shaped stone ruin with a perimeter of 6.5 km. The fort, impressive because of its sheer size, has high gateways, bastioned walls, deep water tanks and the remnants of an underground passage with chambers and a secret escape route. There are 13 gates in all, and seven tanks for water including one which is 15.5 m deep and is nicknamed the 'Jahannum ka Rasta' (Road to Hell). The tallest structure inside the citadel is the Vijay Mandal tower. The ruins of the palace buildings, now overgrown with

LOCATION:
Off Mehrauli-Badarpur Road, on the southern outskirts of Delhi

thorn bushes, hint at the grandeur of the Tughlaqabad Fort in its heyday.

South of the fortress, facing it across a busy causeway, is the mausoleum of Ghiyas ud-din Tughlaq. This red sandstone building with a marble dome and sloping walls is a significant specimen of early Muslim architecture in Delhi. The Tughlaq buildings are almost puritanical in their simplicity and are devoid of ornamentation, compared to the elaborate design preferred by the Lodhis who ruled Delhi many years later. It is the vast dimensions of the Tughlaq monuments, typically built in solid stone and plastered rubble, that give them their characteristic aspect of impenetrable power. The tomb, located in the middle of what once was an artificial lake, houses the cenotaphs of Ghiyas ud-din, his wife and Muhammad bin Tughlaq. A kilometre south-east of the Tughlaqabad Fort lies Adilabad Fort, built by Muhammad bin Tughlaq.

A magnificent 14th century edifice that suffered premature dereliction.

YAMUNA RIVER

The Yamuna, which flows through Delhi, is a sacred river deeply intertwined with the life of the Hindu God Krishna. Legend has it that baby Krishna fell into the Yamuna while he was leaving Mathura, where he was born, in the arms of his father Vasudeva. Later, as a young boy, Krishna regularly played in the waters of the river in the holy city of Vrindavan, where he spent his childhood.

According to Hindu mythology, the Yamuna River, a major tributary of the sacred Ganges, is named after the Hindu Goddess Yamuna, who was the daughter of Surya, the Sun God, and the sister of Yama, the God of Death. Because of the river's association with Yama, it is believed that a dip in it will leave a person enriched and fearless about death. The Yamuna originates from the Yamunotri glacier in the lower Himalayan mountains and stretches for a scenic 1,370 km, flowing through the northern Indian states of Uttaranchal, Uttar Pradesh where Mathura and Vrindavan are located, and Haryana until it reaches Delhi where it extends for about 22 km.

The Yamuna River was once the lifeline of the Indian capital, and occupied an important place in its history. It was on the river's

Once the lifeline of the capital, the Yamuna is now choked with waste and effluents.

banks that places of worship belonging to different religious communities were built in ancient times. Later, Delhi's Islamic rulers chose to build citadels such as Firoz Shah Kotla and the Red Fort, and monuments such as Humayun's Tomb on its banks. In the 1900s, the memorials of the father of the nation Mahatma Gandhi, and Prime Ministers Jawaharlal Nehru, Indira Gandhi and Rajiv Gandhi were established at their cremation sites near the Yamuna, while the 21st century has seen the building of the magnificent Hindu Akshardham Temple in the area.

Where once Delhi lay on the west bank of the Yamuna, in present day, the river cuts through the centre, dividing the city into east and west. The area east of the river, which has grown rapidly in the 1980s and 1990s, is now identified as trans-Yamuna, home to one-third of the city's residents. Unfortunately, due to the ravages of pollution and over-population, the Delhi segment of this holy river is dying, and a major government drive is underway to salvage it. The waters of the river, that gave sustenance to the city, are choking with waste and effluents, and are no longer fit for bathing, let alone drinking. But with government officials promising a complete clean-up by 2010 in time for the Delhi Commonwealth Games, residents are hopeful that the river will eventually be restored to its former glory.